WILD FLOWERS

OF BRITAIN AND EUROPE

FIELD NATURALIST'S LIBRARY

WILD FLOWERS

OF BRITAIN AND EUROPE

ANDREW BRANSON

INTRODUCED BY

TONY SOPER

WHSMITH
EXCLUSIVE
· BOOKS ·

This edition produced exclusively for
W H Smith

Published in 1991 by Hamlyn Publishing Group Limited,
part of Reed International Books,
Michelin House,
81 Fulham Road,
London SW3 6RB

ISBN 0-600-57080-0

Produced by Mandarin Offset

Printed and bound in Hong Kong

Colour Artwork by Roger Gorringe and Ann Davies

Photographic Acknowledgements

Bob Gibbons, 26; Nature Photographers: Robin Bush, 151, Jean Hall, 96, Paul Sterry, 18; Octopus Publishing Group: A Davies, 39, 55, 92, 103, 119, 148, 154, G. du Feu, 29, 45, 54, 65, 125, Bob Gibbons, 9, 11, 13, 16–17, 48–49, 86–87, 110–111, 120–121, 128–129, P. Loughran, 64, 75, 114.

Contents

Introduction by Tony Soper

The time has long since passed when we all needed to know about wild plants. Which to eat, which to avoid for fear of poisoning; how to prepare a poultice or to keep away flies. Nevertheless, most of us have an urge to name the wild flowers we come across in our everyday lives or on excursions to new places.

A few of our wild flowers are so familiar that we take it for granted that we know their names. Daisy, Dandelion, Primrose, for example, can be recognised and named by people who would deny any knowledge of botany. Three is a good start, and it's surprising how quickly the list will grow if you keep your eyes on the job.

Wherever you are, at whatever time of year, some flowers will be 'out', so there is always a chance to put a name to a plant and satisfy a sense of wonder. Although the plants are wild, there is no need to venture into the country. The Red Valerian sprouting from a stone wall or the Dandelion flexing its muscles to widen a crack in the tarmac, are as much of a challenge as the islands of Sea Pinks amid the coastal turf or the purple haze of a Heather moor.

When at first you try to identify an individual flower it presents a puzzling array of personal features. A specific number of petals, a certain colour, a particular arrangement of leaves which may be smooth or hairy or waxy ... but it becomes an individual when you give it a name. More important than that, it is a member of a plant community which thrives in a particular kind of country. So when you start to put names to the flowers you will also, inevitably, learn many other things. It becomes clear, for example, that the low-growing Bilberry, keeping its head down against the wind, grows on open heaths and moors so an expedition to that kind of country will be needed to gather the purple fruits in late summer. If Blackberries satisfy the appetite as well, they can be gathered on almost every kind of land from sea cliff to quarry, woodland to farmland hedge. Sea Lavender grows only by the sea; Yellow Flags need a fresh-watery world. Leaves, latticed by the chomping mouths of caterpillars, lead to exiting discoveries about food plants: that the caterpillar of the White Admiral butterfly feeds on Honeysuckle, and that the much-despised Stinging Nettle is important as a food plant for the Red Admiral. Once you get interested in wild flowers, a host of other interests will flood in. Ivy berries give food to blackbirds, sundews eat insects for breakfast.

There is no doubt about the scientific fascination of wild flowers, but many people seek their company for the pure joy of the experience. The first glimse of a Primrose heralds the spring and lifts the spirits. The shimmering pink of an island clothed in Thrift prints an unforgettable image of sea and seabird summers. The eerie glow of dense Bluebells in a dark wood, is so different from the bright and breezy feeling of the same plant when it clothes the cliffs.

Flowers appeal to our senses in so many different ways that they are bound to have a place in our emotions. Sight usually comes first, like the carpet of Bluebells or Wild Daffodils. But scent is heady stuff. Honeysuckle, breathed in on a summer evening, is as unforgettable as the pungent smell of Wild Garlic with its starry white flowers and thin green leaves. The feel of a plant is important, too, whether it is the unwelcome prick of bramble thorn, the delightful stickiness of Goosegrass seeds or the springy strength of Heather underfoot.

The most powerful sensations are usually provided by flowers in a mass, exhibiting their natural growth. A single Primrose is not particularly inspiring, but the spring-time vista of green and yellow gives a completely new dimension. The humble plant is raised to a new status.

The Primrose season is over all too quickly, and so it is with most wild flowers. So, unlike trees, with their monumental sense of permanence, most flowers have a short moment of perfection, an ephemeral beauty which is the more appreciated when you learn about their habits and seasons. So it is important to take your chance and identify a flower when you see it or risk waiting for another year when its appointed time will come around again.

Tony Soper

GENERAL INTRODUCTION

'I know a bank whereon the wild thyme blows,
Where oxlips and the nodding violet grows
Quite over-canopied with luscious woodbine
With sweet musk-roses, and with eglantine.'

When Shakespeare described this bank in Midsummer Night's Dream in the late 16th Century, it is quite probable that most of his contemporaries not only knew the plants he was describing but would know of such a place themselves. Today, many people would probably find difficulty in describing the plants yet alone know where to find them. Yet for thousands of years our lives have been intimately associated with wild flowers, whether it was simply knowing which were poisonous, or edible, sweet-smelling or would provide a herbal tonic, as well as perhaps, more sinisterly, which were associated with goblins and witches and would bring ill fortune if picked or brought into the home. An understanding of our native flora was as important as our current knowledge of the supermarket.

Thankfully, we have still not lost our love of and curiosity about plants. The hundreds of thousands of avid gardeners testify to that, but we have, to some degree, lost the special relationship that we once had with wild plants. Outside the garden, a knowledge of flowers is all too often thought of as the preserve of biologists or farmers and yet there can be few more arresting sights than a woodland glade full of Primroses and violets, spangled with Wood Anemones, or a cliff side decked out in a mantle of Thrift and Sea Campion.

Although, perhaps partly as a consequence of this break in our understanding of the natural world, we have lost vast amounts of our flower-filled wild landscapes to intensive agriculture and development during the present century, the plant kingdom is still accessible and rewarding to study.

A first step to discovering the wealth of flowers that can be found in Britain and Europe is to be confident in identifying the more common species and this is the main purpose of this guide.

There are approximately 2,000 species of wild flowers in Britain and northern Europe which, while not as large a some of the tropical areas, is still enough to make putting a name to even the more common plants seem daunting. However, unlike some natural history pursuits, you do not have to go to remote areas or even your local nature reserve to make a start as plants have been able to adapt to the most urban of settings. Any untended patch of soil will quickly become colonised and the local park is often a good place to make a start.

Furthermore, to identify most plants there is no need for any equipment at all, other than a guide. It can be useful to have a hand lens or magnifying glass (x8 or x10 magnification) to see some of the finer details, such as the lobes on a calyx or the hairiness of a stem, which can be important for some groups such as the forget-me-nots and speedwells.

This guide describes 280 wild flowers and concentrates on those species that are likely to be encountered and have a wide distribution within the region. For ease of use, I have not included the grasses, sedges and rushes as, although these are every bit as intriguing as the more colourful plants, they can be confusing and are best tackled when one has gained some confidence in identification.

The species are grouped into six main habitats, so plants that are likely to be found growing together are in the same part of the guide. Within the habitats, the plants are arranged conventionally according to their families, with the most primitive plants first. This is the order used in most literature and is quite easy to follow after a while. A box next to each species shows the typical flowering period of the plant.

Cliffs flowers in the spring on Guernsey. The cliffs here are mantled in a tapestry of Bluebells, Sea Campion, and Gorse.

CLASSIFICATION

The plant kingdom is the basis for all life on Earth as only plants, with their chlorophyll or green matter, are able to convert the sun's energy, carbon dioxide and water into living cells which are the basis of the food chain. This immensely important kingdom comprises 17 major divisions including at one end the bacteria, algae, fungi, lichens, mosses and liverworts, ferns, and at the other the flowering plants. This last group consists of two major divisions: the Gymnosperms (meaning 'naked seeds'), consisting largely of the conifers; and the Angiosperms (meaning 'enclosed seeds') which includes the plants with typical flowers and therefore the plants described in this guide.

The Angiosperms are further divided into two main groups: the dicotyledons and the monocotyledons. Essentially a cotyledon is a leaf-like structure that nourishes the germinating seed embryo. The two groups are usually quite distinctive – the dicotyledons have leaves with a complex structure of veins and grow from the tip, whilst the monocotyledons usually have parallel leaf-veins and grow from the base. A rose is a dicotyledon and a Bluebell is a monocotyledon. Below this, plants are divided into orders and families. At this level it can be useful to be aware of the relationships as members of each family often have distinctive features which can help to identify a plant. Plants with closely related characters are grouped into a genus and then each type is a species. Each plant has a scientific or Latin name which includes its genus and species names so, for example, Meadow Buttercup has the genus name of *Ranunculus*, which it shares with other closely-related buttercups, and the specific name of *acris*. It is important to be aware of these names as the common names are often used imprecisely and can lead to confusion, for example, in some areas the plant referred to as the Bluebell is *Campanula rotundifolia*, also known as the Harebell, and not *Hyacinthoides non-scripta*, the Bluebell that carpets our woods in spring!

When birdwatching, it is better to make field notes and then look at your guide later as the bird is likely to disappear. However, with plants it is better to take the book to the plant, where you can study it in detail and check on any particular points you may not have noticed at first glance. Below is a simple guide to the families to help you find the right area in the guide. If in doubt, there is nothing wrong with thumbing through until you find an illustration which looks similar to the flower you are trying to identify.

GUIDE TO FAMILIES

DICOTYLEDONS

Buttercup family – usually 5 petals, many stamens and no stipules *woodlands p.18-19, meadows p.50-1, waterside p.88-9*
Water-lily family – large aquatic plants with floating leaves and flowers with numerous petals and stamens *waterside p.90*
Poppy family – large showy flowers with 4 petals, exuding a white or yellowish juice *coast p.121, man-made p.130*
Fumitory family – flower shaped like a tube with a spur, and waxy green, finely-divided leaves *man-made p.133*
Crucifer or Cabbage family – 4 petals, often arranged in a cross-like shape, 4 sepals usually 6 stamens; seeds in a pod *woodlands p.21, meadows p.52, waterside p.91, man-made p.131-2*
Violet family – small plants with pansy-shaped flowers, 5 petals and 5 sepals *woodlands p.20, man-made p.132*
Milkwort family – low plants with blue or white flowers, 3 petals and 5 sepals, tiny bell-shaped flowers *meadows p.54*
St John's-wort family – yellow flowers with 5 petals, 5 sepals, many stamens *meadows, p.53*
Rock-rose family – low shrub with opposite strap-shaped leaves, 5 petals, 5 sepals, many stamens *meadows p.52*

An unimproved meadow in Ireland dominated by Marsh Marigold and Ragged Robin

Campion family – plants with opposite, usually oval- to strap-shaped leaves, 4-5 petals and sepals often joined at the base to form a calyx, 3-5 styles *woodland p.21-2, meadows p.54-5, coasts p.122, man-made p.133-5*
Goosefoot family – tiny greenish flowers, no petals, 5 sepals, 2-5 stamens, plant often greyish-green *coast p.122, man-made p.136-6*
Mallow family – large showy pink flowers, with a double calyx, 5 petals and many stamens fused at the base *man-made p.136*
Flax family – 5 petals and sepals, 5 stamens, narrow leaves *meadows p.56*
Geranium family – low to medium plants with attractive pink or purple flowers, 5 petals and sepals, 10 stamens, seed capsule is beak-shaped *woods p.23, meadows p.56-7, coasts p.124*
Wood Sorrel family – trefoil leaves, 5 petals, sepals, styles, 10 stamens, fruit 5-angled capsule *woods p.23*
Pea family – 5 petals forming distinctive standard and keel of sweet pea flower, seeds are in a long bean-like pod *woods p.24, meadows p.57-62, heaths p.112, man-made p.137*
Rose family – variable characteristics but usually with divided or pinnate alternate leaves, flowers have their parts in 5s or 4s and fruits often fleshy e.g. strawberry or blackberry *woods p.24-6, meadows p.62-4, waterside p.92-3, heaths p.113, man-made p.137-8*
Stonecrop family – low, succulent plants, 5 petals and sepals, 5 or 10 stamens *coast p.124-5, man-made p.139*
Saxifrage family – low growing with 5 petals and sepals, 10 stamens but golden-saxifrages have no petals, 4 sepals, 8 stamens *meadows p.64, waterside p.84, heaths p.114*
Currant family – shrubs with 5 petals and sepals, 2 styles, berry and palmate leaves *woods p.26*
Sundew family – insectivorous with sticky globular hairs on rosette of leaves, 5-8 petals, sepals and stamens *heaths p.113*
Loosestrife family – flowers with 6 petals, sepals and stamens, leaves opposite or in whorls *waterside p.95*
Willowherb family – usually upright medium to tall plants usually with bright flowers, flower parts in 4s (willowherbs) or 2s (Enchanter's Nightshade) *woods p.27, waterside p.95, man-made p.140*
Water starwort family – small water plants consisting of rosettes of floating or submerged spoon-shaped to linear leaves, tiny flowers *waterside p.96*
Mistletoe family – parasitic shrub with spoon-shaped evergreen leaves and sticky white berries *woods p.30*
Ivy family – woody, evergreen climber with glossy palmate leaves, 5 petals and sepals

woods p.30
Carrot or parsley family – usually upright plants with pinnate or divided leaves, flowers in distinctive umbrella-like heads, 5 petals, 5 stamens, 2 stigmas
woods p.28-9, meadows p.65-6, waterside p.96-8, coasts p.125, man-made p.140-1
Gourd family – one species in region - White Bryony, a climber with palmate leaves and red berries *woods p.29*
Spurge family – low to medium predominantly green plants with no petals but conspicuous green bracts (on spurges), exude a milky juice *woods p.31, man-made p.141*
Dock family – a variable family with usually simple leaves and dense heads of tiny flowers, petals none, sepals 3-6 *meadows p.67, waterside p.98, man-made p.141-3*
Nettle family – small to medium-tall plants often with stinging hairs, simple leaves and small petal-less green flowers, stamens 4-5 *man-made p.144*
Hop family – climbing plants with palmate leaves and cone-like fruits *woods p.31*
Heath and Crowberry families – low shrubs with usually evergreen leaves, 4-5 petals and sepals, tube- or bell-shaped flowers *heaths p.114-6*
Sea-lavender family – simple leaves in basal rosette, flowers tubular, flower parts in 5s *coast p.126*
Primrose family – low growing plants with leaves usually in a basal rosette, attractive yellow or pink flowers, parts in 5s *woods p.32, meadows p.67, waterside p.99, man-made p.144*
Gentian and Bog-bean families – low to medium plants with flowers in branching spike, attractive flowers in an upright lobed corolla *meadows p.68-9, waterside p.99*
Borage and forget-me-not families – medium to tall often bristly plants with flower parts in 5s, usually in an unfurling spike *woods p.33, meadows p.69-70, waterside p.100*
Bindweed family – climbing or trailing plants with trumpet-shaped flowers, 5 sepals *woods p.33, heaths p.117, man-made p.145*
Nightshade family – low to medium-sized plants, often poisonous, with flower parts in 5s, fruit often a berry *woods p.34, man-made p.145*
Figwort and speedwell family – low to tall plants, with flowers often a spike with two-lipped corolla or 4-lobed (speedwells) *woods p.34-6, meadows p.70-2, waterside p.101-2, heaths p.118, man-made p.146-8*

Broomrape family – parasitic plants with an upright stem and leaves reduced to scales, flowers a tube-like corolla *man-made p.148*
Butterwort family – insectivorous plants with an attractive lobed corolla, leaves either in a basal rosette (butterworts) or divided and aquatic (bladderworts) *waterside p.102-3*
Verbena family – only one native species in the region, Vervain, which is a medium plant with spikes of lilac 2-lipped flowers *meadows p.72*
Labiate or mint family – low to medium plants with 2-lipped corollas often in whorls; usually 4 stamens, often aromatic when bruised *woods p.36-9, meadows p.73-4, waterside p.103-4, man-made p.149-50*
Plantain family – low plants with a basal rosette of leaves and a leafless flowering spike with many tiny flowers whose parts are in 4s *meadows p.74-5, coasts p.127, man-made p.150*
Bellflower family – short to tall plants with alternate simple leaves and usually blue bell-shaped flowers, 5 stamens *woods p.39, meadows p.75*
Bedstraw family – short to medium often trailing plants with 4-angled stems and simple leaves in whorls, corollas with 4 lobes *woods p.40, meadows p.75, heaths p.118, man-made p.151*
Honeysuckle family – woody climbers or shrubs with opposite leaves, 5-lobed corolla tube, 5 stamens, fruit berry-like *woods p.41*
Moschatel family – only one species – a low-growing plant with 2-foliate leaves and small green flowers arranged in a right-angled 5-flowered head *woods p.41*
Valerian family – short to tall plants with divided leaves and flowers in a dense panicle, flowers often 5-lobed corolla *waterside p.105, man-made p.152*
Teasel and scabious family – medium to tall plants with opposite simple or pinnate leaves and dense, usually purple flowerheads, 4-5 lobed corolla tube with 2 or 4 protruding stamens *woods p.42, meadows p.76*
Composite or daisy family – largest family of flowering plants in the world. Low to tall plants with tiny tube-like flowers combined into a dense disc-like or globular flowerhead often consisting of inner florets and outer strap-like ray florets, seeds often have a pappus of hairs to assist in wind-borne dispersal
woods p.42-3, meadows p.77-83, waterside p.105-6, coasts p.127, man-made p.152-7

A late summer dispaly of Autumn Crocus and Hedge Bedstraw

MONOCOTYLEDONS

Water-plantain family – aquatic plants with 3 sepals and 3 white petals *waterside p.107*
Pondweed family – aquatic plants with often floating oval or strap-shaped leaves and greenish flowers in a dense cylindrical spike *waterside p.109*
Lily family – bulbous plants usually with strap-shaped or oval leaves and flower parts in 6s, the ovary is inferior *woods p.43-5, 47*
Iris family – similar to the above but with superior ovary and 3 stamens *waterside p.109*
Yam family – only one native species in the region, Black Bryony, a climbing deciduous plant with arrow-shaped leaves and 3 sepals and petals, berry-like fruit *woods p.45*
Orchid family – large family with attractive often complex flowers, short to medium plants with strap-shaped or oval leaves *woods p.46, meadows p.84-5, heaths p.119*
Arum family – medium to tall plants with a complex dense flowering spike in Arum surrounded by a cowl-like spathe *woods p.47*
Duckweed family – tiny floating on submerged plants consisting chiefly of a leaf-like frond with minute greenish flowers *waterside p.109*

GLOSSARY

annual a plant which flowers and dies within one year, e.g. Common Poppy
anther the top of the stamen which produces pollen
berry a fleshy fruit with numerous, hard-coated seeds, e.g. White Bryony
biennial a plant which takes two years to complete its life cycle, producing leaves in the first year, flowering and then dying in the second, e.g. Foxglove
bract a small leaf, green or scale-like, either at the base of a flower stalk or grouped beneath a flowerhead
bulb an enlarged, underground bud with fleshy, scale-like leaves
calyx the sepals either separate or joined
capsule a dry fruit with compartments which splits open releasing the seeds
compound (of leaf) divided into separate leaflets
corolla the petals either separate or joined
deciduous any part of the plant shed at the end of a season, usually the leaves
dicotyledon a plant of the major group which is characterised by having two seed leaves, flower parts mostly in fours or fives and usually broad, net-veined leaves
dioecious having male and femal flowers on separate plants e.g. Stinging nettle
epicalyx a circle of small, leafy structures borne outside the calyx
floret a small, often tubular, flower which forms part of a compound head as in the family Compositae
irregular describes flowers which are bilaterally symmetrical, that is, which can be cut into equal halves in only one plane, from front to back
latex a milky juice, white or coloured
leaflet a separate segment of a leaf which often resembles a leaf but has no associated bud or stipule

lobed divided, but not into separate parts
monocotyledon a plant of the major group which is characterised by having one seed leaf, flower parts mostly in threes, and usually narrow leaves with parallel viens
node a junction on a stem where one or more leaf stalks join it
nutlet a small, single-seeded fruit with a hard coat
ochrea a delicate sheath encircling the stem just above a leaf
ovary the central part of the flower containing the ovules which later develop into seeds
palmate having leaflets radiating from the same point
pappus a circle of hairs, bristles, or scales (representing the calyx) at the top of the ovary of flowers of the daisy family (Compositae)
perennial a plant which lives for more than two years, usually flowering in each year
petal a segment of the corolla, often brightly coloured
pinnate bearing leaflets along each side of the leaf axis
pod a long, dry cylindrical fruit which splits open releasing the seeds, often flattened in cross-section e.g. a pea
pollen fine dust-like substance produced by the anthers, containing male 'sperm' which fertilise the ovules
ray floret florets at the edge of the flowerhead of a plant of the daisy family in which the corolla is either expanded on one side to produce a strap-shaped 'petal', or larger than the inner florets
reflexed curled or bent abruptly at more than a right angle
regular describes flowers which are radially symmetrical
rhizome a creeping underground stem, often swollen with food reserves, from which grow leaves and stems each year
rosette a radiating cluster of leaves, usually lying close to the ground e.g. Dandelion
saprophyte a plant which lacks chlorphyll and lives by absorbing food from decaying organic matter

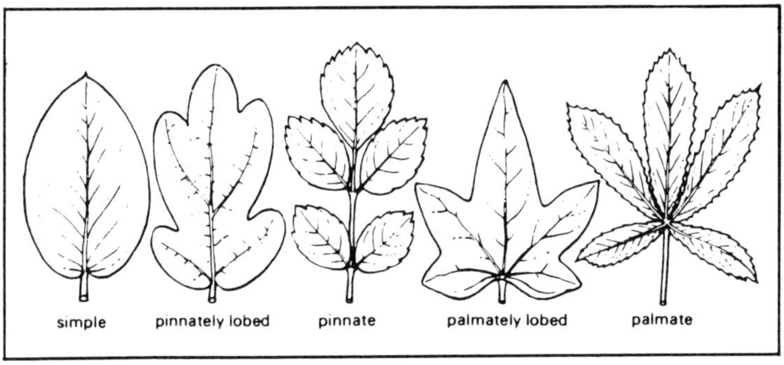

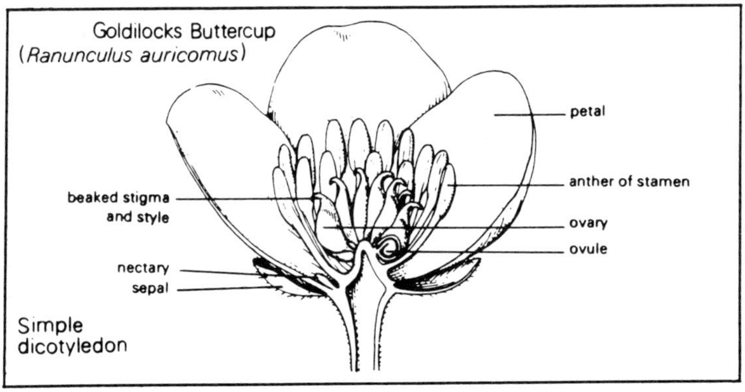

scale a papery or woody flap of tissue, usually a much-reduced leaf
sepal a segment of the calyx, usually small, green and leaf-like
simple leaves that are undivided or not compound
spur a long, normally nectar-producing projection from a sepal or petal e.g. violets
stamen the male reproductive structure, usually stalked, with an anther at the tip
stigma the receptive part of the ovary, varying in form, on which the pollen is received
stipule a leafy outgrowth, paired and varying in shape, which develops from the leaf base
style a prolongation of the ovary, varying in shape, which develops from the leaf base
style a prolongation of the ovary which bears the stigma(s)
tendril a coil-like extension of a leaf, which twines around supporting vegetation
trifoliate with three leaflets, as in a clover leaf
tuber a swollen, underground stem or root
umbel an umbrella-shaped arrangement with the flower stalks arising from a common point, e.g. carrot family
whorl a ring of three or more similar structures, usually leaves

WOODLANDS AND HEDGEROWS

For much of the lowlands of Britain and Europe, woodland is the natural climax vegetation. Before man cleared vast areas for agriculture, the landscape would have been covered in a rich mosaic of woodland types with different species of plant communities, each varying subtly according to the changing soil conditions and the amount of light and shade. Today, woodlands often no longer dominate the scene, in Britain, for example, only about 7% of the land is covered in woods.

However, much of this consists of recently-planted woods, scrub and coniferous plantations. A much smaller percentage is old or ancient woodland that may have a lineage stretching back to the end of the last ice age. It is in these ancient woods that the greatest variety of woodland plants can be found and because many of these have poor powers of dispersal, in some regions particular flowers are only found in these woodlands.

The way a wood has been traditionally managed can have a marked effect on the wild flowers. Woods that have areas regularly cut or coppiced (cutting the shoots back to ground level every 10-15 years) are more open in appearance and may have carpets of violets, primroses and other light-loving plants, whilst areas which have been traditionally grazed may have a woodland floor community dominated by grasses. Overgrown woods or high forest, which has a denser canopy, will have more shade-tolerant plants.

Soil type plays an important part in determining the range of plants. In dry, calcareous woodlands the ground flora may be dominated by plants such as Dog's Mercury. On more acid soils, Wood Sorrel and Bluebells may dominate. On poorly-drained clay soils, look out for Ramsons and Lesser Celandine.

Old hedgerows may also be linked to former woods and have a rich flora. More recent ones can still harbour a wide range of plants that require shade and more sheltered conditions.

A carpet of Ramsons growing in an old hazel coppice

STINKING HELLEBORE

Helleborus foetidus

Characteristics: An early-flowering perennial, growing up to 80cm. This robust plant has long-stalked, dark green lower leaves which overwinter. These are divided into 3 to 9 radiating segments with toothed edges. The upper plant is often very branched with smaller, undivided, paler bracts and clusters of drooping, bell-shaped, yellow-green flowers made up of sepals tinged purple at the tips. Pollinated by early-flying bees, but the seeds are later dispersed by wandering snails. The plant has a fetid smell.

Range and habitat: An uncommon plant of dry chalk and limestone woods on thin soils in southern Britain, becoming increasingly rare towards the north. It is found throughout southern and central Europe north to Belgium. Most typical of beechwoods.

Similar species: In some areas, the Green Hellebore, *H. viridis*, can also be found. This is more typical of damper woods and has flat, open flowers, deciduous lower leaves and divided, toothed upper leaves (bracts).

JAN	FEB	MAR	APR	MAY	JUN	JULY	AUG	SEPT	OCT	NOV	DEC

WOOD ANEMONE

Anemone nemorosa

Characteristics: A delicate woodland perennial, up to 30cm high, with striking white flowers borne singly on a long stalk. The flower half closes and droops when it is overcast, reacting quickly to sunlight by becoming erect and opening out its 6 or 7 petal-like segments to display a mass of yellow anthers at its centre. The underside of the flower can sometimes be flushed pink-purple. Two-thirds up the stem is a whorl of 3 deeply-divided, palmate, dark green leaves that are often the only trace of the flower to be found by late spring.

Range and habitat: It is found throughout most of Britain, Ireland and continental Europe. It is a typical plant of semi-natural woods and old hedgebanks, although it can be found in alpine meadows on the Continent. It spreads by a network of underground rhizomes, gradually colonising large areas of woodland to produce the familiar white carpets of flowers.

Similar species: None.

JAN	FEB	MAR	APR	MAY	JUN	JULY	AUG	SEPT	OCT	NOV	DEC

TRAVELLER'S JOY

Clematis vitalba

Characteristics: A familiar perennial woody climber which festoons shrubs and trees. It can grow up to 30m, the stem becoming woody with a fibrous bark. The leaf usually consist of 3 to 5 toothed leaflets, the stalk of which can wind itself around the branches of the supporting trees or shrubs. The scented flower is made up of 4 pale green sepals, downy on the outside, with numerous yellow stamens. The distinctive fruits, which give the plant its other name of 'Old Man's Beard', consist of small nutlets with long, silky plumes. They are at their best in October and can form a dense, white mantle over hedgerows and scrub in chalk and limestone districts.

Range and habitat: It is a native plant in Britain south from Yorkshire and Lancashire and has been widely naturalized in Ireland. In Europe it is widespread south of the Netherlands. It is confined to calcareous soils where it can be very common, scrambling over trees and shrubs.

Similar species: None in the wild.

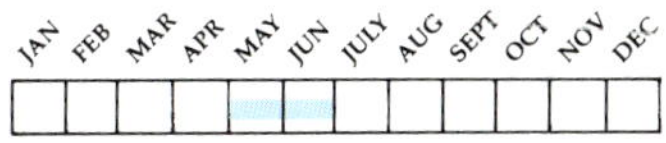

COLUMBINE

Aquilegia vulgaris

Characteristics: The intriguingly-shaped pendent flowers of this perennial have attracted the attention of man for many centuries. As a result, various species and cultivars are now widely grown as garden plants. The wild plant is a grey-green colour and can grow up to 1m tall. The long-stalked lower leaves have deep, rounded lobes. The hanging flowers are large (3-5cm), made up of 5 petals each with a long, curving tubular spur and 5 sepals, all a deep blue-violet colour. The fruits are erect, looking like a 5-pointed jester's hat.

Range and habitat: It is probably native in Britain as far north as the Scottish lowlands and grows locally in Ireland. Found throughout most of Europe. A local plant of woodland and damp places.

Similar species: None.

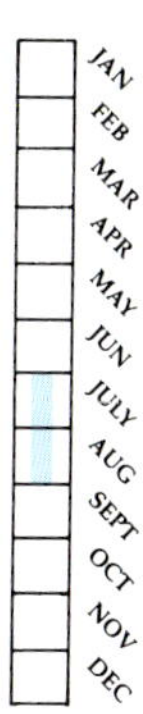

SWEET VIOLET

Viola odorata

Characteristics: This delightful plant is one of the earliest to flower amongst the hedgebanks and woodland edges, its deep violet petals standing out amidst a mass of glossy, heart-shaped leaves. It spreads by means of creeping runners or stolons, from which grow the long-stalked leaves and flowers. Most of the other woodland violets are hairless, while this one sometimes has downy stalks and leaves. It is not unusual to find colonies of white-flowered forms, but purple and pink ones are more uncommon.

Range and habitat: A rare plant in Scotland, becoming commoner southwards. Common throughout Europe. It is found in hedgebanks, woods, plantations and scrub, usually on calcareous soils, often as a garden escape.

Similar species: This is the only woodland violet with scented flowers.

COMMON DOG VIOLET

Viola riviniana

Characteristics: When walking through woodland in the spring, this is the violet that is most likely to be encountered. When in flower, it can be readily distinguished by its curved spur, which is blunt-tipped and paler than the rest of the irregular, 5-petalled flower. The overall colour of the flower is blue-violet, with dark purple veins on the lower lip. The leaves are heart-shaped, and only slightly longer than they are wide. As with most violets, the spring flower rarely sets seed and later in summer the plant puts out another flower which never fully opens and is self-fertilising.

Range and habitat: Found throughout Britain, Ireland and most of Europe. A common plant of woodland rides and clearings, hedgebanks, heaths, moors and even rocky mountain slopes.

Similar species: In calcareous woodlands another violet, the Early Dog Violet, *V. reichenbachiana*, can be quite common, except in north and west Britain. It has slightly paler, narrower flowers, with a darker straight spur.

GARLIC MUSTARD

Allaria petiolata

Characteristics: A common biennial plant, also known as 'Jack-by-the-hedge'. It grows in distinctive groups made up of single, unbranched, upright stems growing up to 120cm. Easily picked out by its large, toothed, bright green leaves which are heart-shaped at the base, becoming triangular further up the stem. The plant is topped with a small head of white flowers, each with 4 distinct petals arranged in the typical cross-shape of the Cruciferae family. The long, curved fruits are 4-angled and erect, up to 60mm long. The tap root and lower leaves smell of garlic when bruised.

Range and habitat: Found throughout the British Isles, becoming scarce in north Scotland and parts of Ireland. It is common in central and northern Europe. A common plant of shady hedgebanks, woodland edges and open deciduous woods on calcareous soils.

Similar species: Told from other white-flowered members of the cabbage family by the garlic smell and large, toothed leaves.

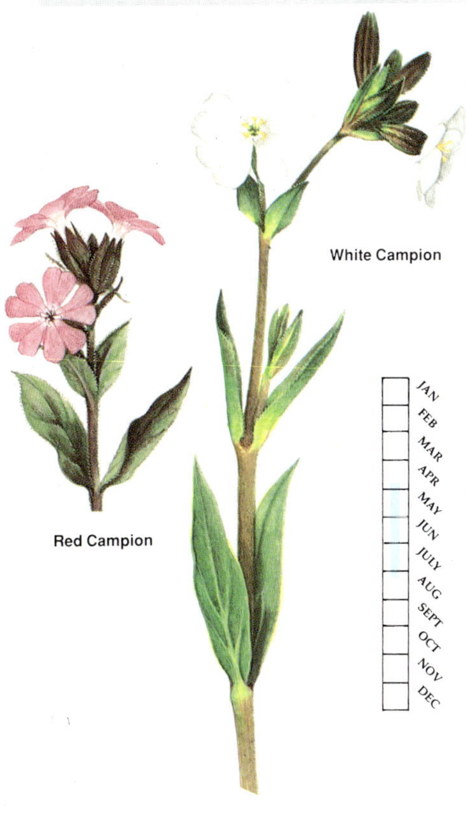

RED CAMPION

Silene dioica

Characteristics: West County hedgebanks in early summer are spangled with the rose-red flowers of Red Campion. This short-lived perennial (up to 100cm tall) has a downy stem and spear-shaped leaves which grow in opposite pairs. The branched inflorescence contains several flowers which have deeply forked petals protruding from a sticky calyx tube. There are separate male and female plants, the female flowers have 5 styles and the males have 10 stamens.

Range and habitat: It is most common in south and west Britain. It is very local in Ireland. Widespread throughout Europe. It is a classic plant of shady hedgebanks and wood edges on base-rich soils.

Similar species: The closely-related White Campion, *S. alba*, is similar in appearance but has larger white flowers. When the two grow together, pink-flowered hybrids can be found. It is fragrant and opens in the evening to be pollinated by moths. It is more typical of open habitats in the east.

GREATER STITCHWORT

Stellaria holostea

Characteristics: This woodland perennial has weak, square stems which are supported by the woodland grasses and herbs that it grows amongst. Look out for its star-like white flowers amongst the Bluebells in May. The rough-edged leaves are narrow and spear-shaped, joined at the base, and growing in opposite pairs along the stem, each pair at right angles to the next. The 5 petals are divided halfway down into 2 lobes, and are noticeably longer than the sepals. The whole flower is up to 30mm across.

Range and habitat: It is found throughout most of Britain and Ireland. It is also widespread in Europe, except the far south and north. A very common plant of shady woodlands, hedgebanks and woodland edges.

Similar species: Told from Lesser Stitchwort by its larger flowers and leaves. Bog Stitchwort, *S. alsine*, which can also be found along damp woodland rides, is much smaller with the pointed sepals extending beyond the petals.

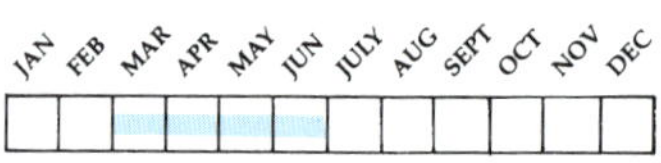

THREE-VEINED SANDWORT

Moehringia trinerva

Characteristics: A low, trailing annual with shoots up to 40cm long. It is closely related to the chickweeds, pearlworts and stitchworts, which can be a confusing group of white-flowered plants. A close look at the leaf and flower should soon clear up any difficulties. The leaves are rather small and the upper ones appear to be joined directly to the stem. If held up to the light you can see 3 clear veins. The petals of the flower are not notched or split. The sepals are longer than the petals. The fruit is shorter than the sepals, unlike other sandworts and pearlworts. It is usually self-pollinating.

Range and habitat: Found throughout the British Isles but is more scarce in Ireland and northern Scotland and is absent from the Orkneys and Shetland. It is widespread in Europe. A plant of woodlands and copses, it is often associated with ancient woodland on well-drained, fertile soils.

Similar species: Told from other small white-flowered plants by the oval, 3-veined leaves and unnotched petals.

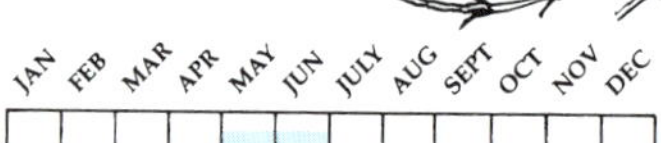

HERB ROBERT

Geranium robertianum

Characteristics: A familiar annual or biennial member of the geranium family, up to 40cm tall. It has hairy, much-branched, leafy stems, the leaves are deeply lobed to the base and can vary in colour from bright green to deep red, particularly in dry, exposed situations. The flower, which is 10-15mm across, has pink, unnotched petals with noticeable veins. The tiny anthers are orange or purple. The fruit, like all geraniums, has a long beak which splits and breaks into 5 sections to release the seeds. The whole plant has a strong 'geranium' smell to it.

Range and habitat: It is almost cosmopolitan in its distribution and is found throughout the British Isles and Europe. A common plant of shady, damp places including woodlands, hedgebanks and waste ground; often found in crevices in old walls and tree stumps or on rocky scree and shingle.

Similar species: Told from the other wild geraniums by the unnotched flowers and broadly triangular outline of the deeply-lobed leaves.

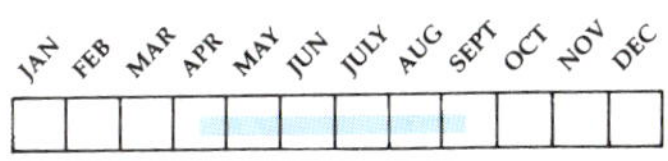

WOOD-SORREL

Oxalis acetosa

Characteristics: A creeping perennial with the leaves and flowers on long stalks (up to 15cm). The leaves are made up of 3, heart-shaped, clover-like leaflets, often hanging. The 5-petalled flowers (10-25mm across) are borne singly; the petals are white and delicately veined with purple. Like the violets, Wood-sorrel produces summer flowers that do not fully open and are self-pollinating. The flowers and leaves are very responsive to both light and movement and will drop down at night or in strong sunlight.

Range and habitat: A common plant of dry woodlands throughout the British Isles. Widespread in Europe. This shade-tolerant plant can often carpet beechwoods with its white flowers.

Similar species: The only native member of the *Oxalis* genus, but there are a number of naturalised species such as the yellow-flowered *O. corniculata*, and the pink-flowered *O. articulata*.

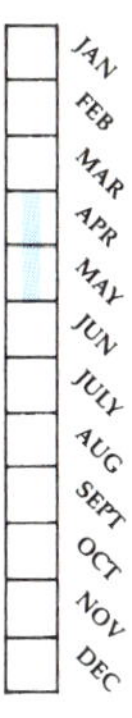

TUFTED VETCH

Vicia cracca

A sprawling perennial of hedgerows and scrub growing up to 200cm amongst other plants. The leaves have between 6 and 12 pairs of lance-shaped, downy leaflets and branched tendrils at the tips. The flowering spikes can have up to 40 bright purple pea-like flowers which produce hairless brown pods.

Range and habitat: It is found throughout the British Isles except for parts of the Scottish Highlands and is widespread throughout Europe. It is a very common plant of hedgebanks and scrub as well as woodland edges, where it twines itself amongst the taller-growing plants and shrubs. It is most typical of broadly neutral soils.

Similar species: Bush Vetch, *V. sepium*, flowers slightly earlier in the year (May-August) and is usually shorter with more or less hairless leaves with 5 to 9 pairs of oval-shaped leaflets and branched tendrils. The flower spike is more compact with up to 6 pale pinkish-purple flowers; the pods are black. It is found in similar habitats.

DOG ROSE

Rosa canina agg.

Characteristics: A low-growing, deciduous shrub (up to 3m) with large, arching stems covered with strongly-hooked prickles. The leaves have 2 to 3 pairs of toothed leaflets with a terminal leaflet. The large (4-5cm), 5-petalled flowers are variable in colour, ranging from white through to pink. The styles are loose and, together with the numerous stamens, form a vivid yellow centre to the bloom. It is visited by many insects for pollen. The distinctive fruit or hip is bright red, oval and can be picked to produce rose-hip syrup which is rich in vitamin C.

Range and habitat: Found throughout the British Isles and Europe. It is a common plant of woodland edges and rides, hedgerows and scrub.

Similar species: The Field Rose, *R. arvensis*, looks similar but is a smaller shrub with less robust stems and smaller prickles. The flowers are always white and the styles are fused together to form a central column. The hip is more rounded. The Field Rose has a more southerly distribution.

BRAMBLE, BLACKBERRY

Rubus fruticosus agg.

Characteristics: A familiar trailing perennial shrub with numerous arching and scrambling stems which often root at the tip. The plant is armed with many sharp, hooked prickles and spines of various sizes. The leaves have 3 to 5 usually hairy leaflets. The flowers have 5 white to pink petals. The fruit or blackberry turns from green to red to a deep, glossy purple-black when ripe. Although most people class blackberries into those that have large, juicy fruits and those with smaller fruits, to the botanist they are much more complex with over 2,000 microspecies in Europe and approximately 400 in the British Isles. This proliferation is due to the fact that they are apomictic (they can set seed without fertilization) though pollination is needed for the fruits to ripen.
Range and habitat: Widespread throughout the British Isles but becoming scarce in northern Scotland. Common in north-west Europe. It is found in hedgerows, scrub, woodland edges and rides, heaths and waste ground.

JAN	FEB	MAR	APR	MAY	JUN	JULY	AUG	SEPT	OCT	NOV	DEC

JAN	FEB	MAR	APR	MAY	JUN	JULY	AUG	SEPT	OCT	NOV	DEC

WILD STRAWBERRY

Frageria vesca

Characteristics: This delightful plant looks like a miniature garden strawberry. It is a low-growing perennial (up to 30cm) producing rooting runners. The leaves have three leaflets which are glossy green above and paler below, with toothed edges. The small, white flowers have 5, unnotched petals and produce a delicious red, fleshy fruit, 1-2cm long.
Range and habitat: Common and widespread throughout the British Isles, except the north of Scotland. It is found throughout Europe. It is a common plant of hedgebanks, scrub, woodland clearings and old pasture, preferring calcareous to neutral soils.
Similar species: The Barren Strawberry, *Potentilla sterilis*, has dull, blue-green leaves; the terminal tooth at the tip of each leaflet is shorter than those on either side, unlike the Wild Strawberry where it is noticeably longer. The 5, notched, white petals are separated so that the green sepals can easily be seen and it does not produce a fleshy fruit, hence the name.

WOOD AVENS, HERB BENNET

Geum urbanum

Characteristics: A distinctive, upright, branched perennial, growing to 60cm. The downy basal leaves are pinnately-lobed with a larger terminal 3-lobed leaflet. The upper leaves and leaf-like stipules are smaller. The 5-petalled, yellow flowers are shorter than the long, arching, green sepals. The clustered fruits have long, hooked styles which catch on the fur of passing animals and the clothes of wandering humans. The name Herb Bennet is derived from the medieval latin *'herba benedicta'*, meaning 'blessed herb'. It is said that the spicy odour of the roots repelled the devil.

Habitat and distribution: It is widely distributed throughout the British Isles and Europe. It prefers damp, slightly acid to calcareous soils, and is a typical plant of woodland rides and hedgebanks and other shady places, usually flowering after most of the other woodland plants.

Similar species: None.

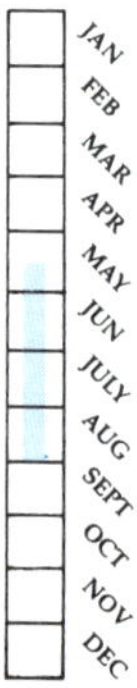

RED CURRANT

Ribes sylvestre

Characteristics: An upright, deciduous shrub growing up to 2m (usually 100-200cm). Leaves 3- to 5-lobed, with the edges blunt-toothed, normally downy, particularly when fresh. They are not strongly aromatic and have heart-shaped bases. The flowers, which grow in a loose spike, consist of a 5-angled green receptable tinged purplish at the edges and with a raised rim. The berries are round and red.

Range and habitat: It is widespread in Britain and Europe, although rarer in Scotland (where it is, to some extent, replaced by the Downy Currant, *R. spicatum*). Rare in Ireland. This is the same species of currant that is grown in gardens and is probably not native across large parts of its range in northwest Europe and Britain as bird-sown seeds readily germinate. It is found along woodland edges, hedgebanks and stream sides.

Similar species: The Black Currant, *R. nigrum,* has strong-smelling, glandular leaves and black fruits.

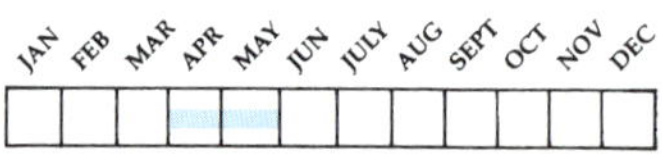

ROSEBAY WILLOWHERB

Epilobium augustifolium

Characteristics: A striking perennial up to 150cm tall, sometimes forming dense stands. It has numerous spirally arranged lance-shaped leaves with wavy edges. The impressive flower spike consists of numerous spreading flowers arranged around the vertical spike. The flowers are 2-3cm across and consist of 4 rose-purple petals with 4 darker sepals in between. The seed capsule eventually becomes erect and can be up to 8cm long. It splits to release numerous plumed seeds which are dispersed by the wind.

Range and habitat: An abundant coloniser of disturbed sites such as railway embankments, fire sites (hence the other name of Fireweed), woodland clearings, waste-tips and scree slopes.

Similar species: Broad-leaved Willowherb, *E. montanum*, is shorter (up to 60cm) with usually opposite-toothed, oval-shaped leaves on short stalks. The smaller, pale pink flowers are in loose, leafy spikes with a distinct white 4-lobed stigma. It is found in woodlands on base-rich soils.

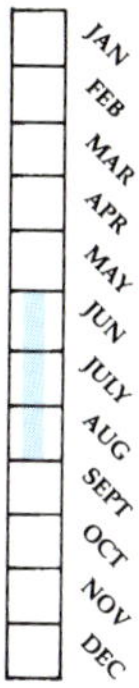

fruit

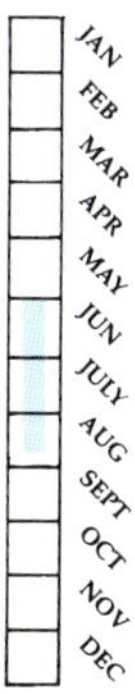

ENCHANTER'S NIGHTSHADE

Circaea lutetiana

Characteristics: An upright perennial (up to 70cm) with opposite, stalked leaves with rounded bases and gradually tapered, pointed tips. Each pair is borne at right-angles to the pair below. The well-spaced flowers are borne on a long spike and consist of 2 white, notched petals (2-4mm long). The fruit are covered in hooked bristles and are club-shaped, clinging on to passing animals. It is thought that the name comes from Circe, the beautiful enchantress that turned Ulysses' crew into pigs.

Range and habitat: It is widespread throughout the British Isles and Europe except for northern Scotland where it is rare or absent. A typical plant of heavily-shaded woods on base-rich soils, where it can form extensive stands, spreading by means of its underground stolens. It also occurs as a weed of garden shrubberies, where it can be difficult to eradicate.

Similar species: The small 2-lipped flowers and habit of this plant are highly distinctive.

SANICLE
Sanicula europaea

Characteristics: A woodland member of the distinctive carrot or parsley family (Umbelliferae). It is a perennial, growing up to 60cm, with 3- to 5-lobed, toothed leaves. They are dark green and shiny, rather like an ivy leaf. The flowers are borne in compact umbels and are white to pale pink. The flowers on the outside of the umbel are male and are stalked; those towards the centre are bisexual and stalkless. The fruits are covered with fine, hooked bristles, enabling them to be dispersed by animals.

Range and habitat: It is found throughout the British Isles except in some highly-cultivated districts, becoming more scarce towards the north of Scotland. It is common throughout Europe in wooded regions. A typical plant of deciduous woods on fertile or base-rich soils. It is very tolerant of shade and can form dense carpets in beechwoods on lime soils.

Similar species: Told from other members of the carrot family by its shiny, ivy-like, palmately-lobed leaves.

COW PARSLEY
Anthriscus sylvestris

Characteristics: A typical member of the carrot or umbel family (Umbelliferae) with large 'plates' of white flowers, looking sometimes rather like a flat-topped umbrella. Cow Parsley is a tall perennial up to 1m high with unspotted stems and bright green, deeply dissected, almost fern-like, leaves. The white flowerhead or umbel is up to 4cm across with 3 to 6 rays. There are no bracts at the base of the flowerhead but there are small bracts (bracteoles) underneath the individual rays. The fruit is smooth, long and wider at the base.

Range and habitat: Common or abundant throughout the British Isles and Europe except for north-west Scotland and western Ireland. Hedgebanks and roadsides can be covered with a white mass of Cow Parsley in May, particularly in southern Britain.

Similar species: Later in the year (July-August) a similar-looking umbel, Upright Hedge-parsley, *Torilis japonica*, comes into flower. This has bracts and bracteoles, and round bristly fruits.

PIGNUT

Conopodium majus

Characteristics: A delicate perennial umbel, easily recognised by its smooth unspotted stem (up to 50cm) and its fine, deeply-divided, feathery leaves, which soon die back. The flowerheads droop in bud but are erect in flower with 6 to 12 rays of white flowers. There are usually no bracts and only a few small bracteoles. The fruit is ridged and oval in shape. The plant arises from a brown, fleshy root tuber up to 3.5cm in diameter. This has traditionally been eaten by pigs, hence the name. It is supposed to be edible raw or cooked.

Range and habitat: It is found throughout the British Isles except in highly-cultivated regions such as the east Midlands; locally common throughout western Europe. A common plant of dry neutral to acid woodlands, old pastures and hay meadows.

Similar species: Great Pignut, *Bunium bulbocastanum*, is a rare plant of chalk grassland in central England. It has similar leaves but has a solid stem and many bracts and bracteoles.

JAN	FEB	MAR	APR	MAY	JUN	JULY	AUG	SEPT	OCT	NOV	DEC

WHITE BRYONY

Bryonia dioica

Characteristics: This climbing perennial is the only wild British species of the mostly tropical gourd family, including such members as the Cucumber and Water-melon. All parts of White Bryony are poisonous. The stem can be very long and branching, enmeshing itself amongst hedgerow shrubs and trees by means of coiled tendrils which are next to the leaf stalk. The leaves are palmately-lobed, rather like a pale ivy leaf. The clusters of yellow-green flowers are either all male or female on a plant as it is dioecious. The female flowers are shorter-stalked and smaller than the male ones. The fruit is a glossy, red berry, which is often left till well into winter, implying it is not the birds' first choice of food.

Range and habitat: Restricted to central and south-eastern England; rare or absent in the rest of the British Isles. Most common in central and southern Europe. It grows in hedgerows and woodland edges on well-drained neutral to basic soils.

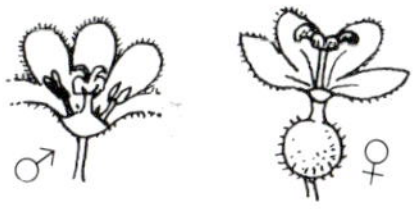

male flower female flower

JAN	FEB	MAR	APR	MAY	JUN	JULY	AUG	SEPT	OCT	NOV	DEC

MISTLETOE
Viscum album

Characteristics: A woody, parasitic evergreen with branching, dull green stems up to 1m long. The pairs of leathery leaves are wider above the middle with blunt tips. The inconspicuous 4-petalled, green flowers are in compact clusters. It is dioecious. The sticky, white berry ripens in November and December. It was a potent force in Druid ceremonies and its magical properties of granting fertility are still echoed today with the Christmas custom of kissing under the Mistletoe.

Range and habitat: It is found throughout England and Wales, becoming less common to the north and west. It is absent from Scotland and Ireland. Common in Europe north to southern Scandinavia. It is most usually found on the branches of deciduous trees, most typically apple, lime and poplar, rarely on oaks.

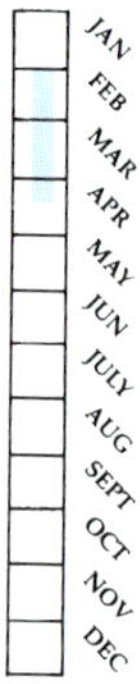

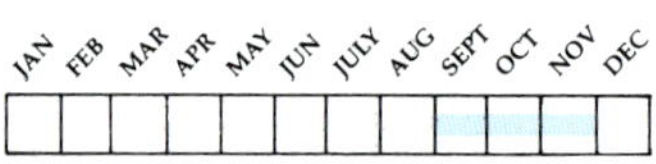

IVY
Hedera helix

Characteristics: A familiar, woody, evergreen climbing plant up to 30m tall, sometimes forming dense mats in new woodland and scrub. The climbing shoots have numerous adhesive roots. The leaves on the non-flowering shoots typically have 5, triangular-shaped lobes whilst the leaves on the flowering parts are more oval in shape, often with wavy edges. The flowers, which grow in round heads, have 5, small, greenish-yellow petals. The flower is highly attractive to flies and wasps. The fruit is ribbed, round and black. The summer brood of the Holly Blue butterfly lays its eggs on the flower buds in August.

Range and habitat: Common throughout the British Isles and the rest of Europe. Ivy can be found growing up trees, rocks, fences, and walls virtually anywhere except in very wet or very acid soils. It is very tolerant of shade.

Similar species: None.

DOG'S MERCURY
Mercurialis perennis

Characteristics: An early flowering perennial which can form dense carpets of plants by means of its long creeping rhizomes. It has erect unbranched stems up to 40cm. The leaves are held in opposite pairs and are oval to elliptical in shape, with finely-toothed edges. The plant is dioecious; the flowers are on upright spikes arising from the leaf axils; they have 3 inconspicuous, green sepals; the female flowers form hairy, round fruits.
Range and habitat: A widespread and sometimes abundant plant of deciduous woodland throughout the British Isles except the north of Scotland. It is very common throughout the Continent. It can dominate the ground flora of beechwoods on chalk and whilst it is confined to old woods in eastern England, it can be found in hedgerows and recent plantations in the west.
Similar species: Annual Mercury, *M. annua*, is a branching and hairless annual. It is a locally common weed species of waste ground.

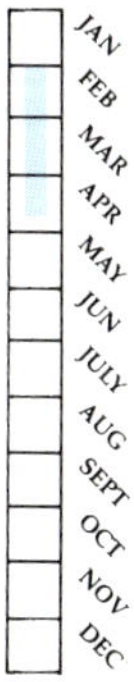

HOP
Humulus lupulus

Characteristics: A climbing perennial, up to 6m long; twists its rough-angled stems clockwise around the branches of surrounding shrubs and trees. The large leaves (up to 15cm) are 3- to 5-lobed with coarse teeth. Dioecious; both male and female flowers are small and greenish-yellow. The male flowers are in clusters and the female flowers form a cone of large papery bracts which enlarge to form the well-known 'hop-flowers' that are used in brewing.
Range and habitat: A native plant of England and Wales northwards to Scotland; rarer in the north of its range. It is widely distributed in most of Europe. Throughout its range it has also escaped from cultivated hop fields. Its native habitat is hedgebanks, scrub and woodland edges on rich soils.

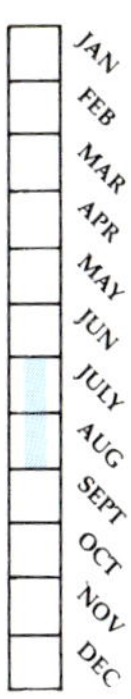

PRIMROSE

Primula vulgaris

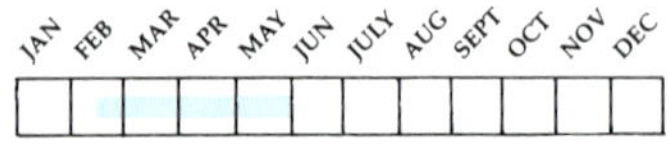

Characteristics: The primrose or 'first rose' is often the true herald of the spring flowering season, as the rosettes of yellow flowers with their bright green leaves blossom along the woodland rides and hedgebanks. This perennial has crinkled, toothed, spoon-shaped leaves, hairless above, narrowing gradually to the base. The open, pale yellow, fine-lobed flowers are carried singly on hairy stalks from the centre of the leaf rosette. The calyx tube is hairy and nearly cylindrical.
Range and habitat: Found throughout the British Isles and western Europe, less common in the north. A typical plant of woodland rides and glades where it can grow in large numbers, also hedgebanks and old grassland.
Similar species: Cowslip, *Primula veris*, has leaves which narrow abruptly, the smaller, deeper yellow flowers are carried in a cluster. Hybrids of the two plants, the False Oxlip, *Primula veris x vulgaris*, can occur but do not confuse with the rare Oxlip, *P. elatior*, a local plant of clay woods in East Anglia.

YELLOW PIMPERNEL

Lysimachia nemorum

Characteristics: A creeping (up to 40cm) perennial with oval, pointed leaves borne in pairs. The small (12mm), yellow, 5-lobed, pimpernel-like flower is carried on a long stalk (longer than the leaves); the calyx-teeth are narrow and spreading.
Range and habitat: A widespread and common plant throughout the British Isles, except in Shetland and parts of the east Midlands. Found in western and central Europe. A characteristic plant of damp woodland rides and hedgebanks on neutral to mildly acid soils.
Similar species: Creeping Jenny, *L. nummularia*, is found in similar habitats. It has blunter, almost rounded leaves and the larger, bell-shaped, yellow flowers with overlapping caylx-teeth, held on more robust stalks that are shorter than the leaves.

Creeping Jenny

Yellow Pimpernel

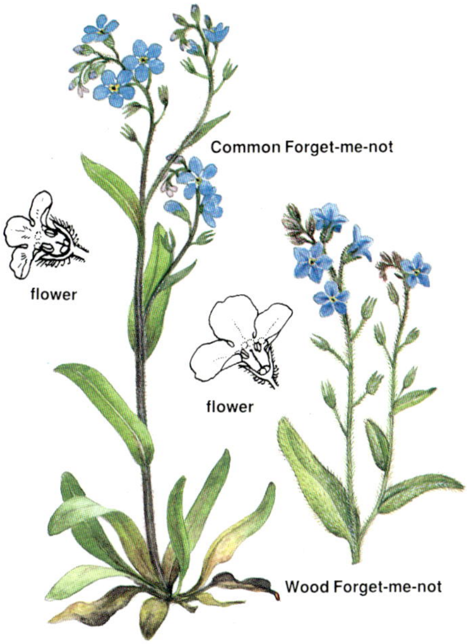

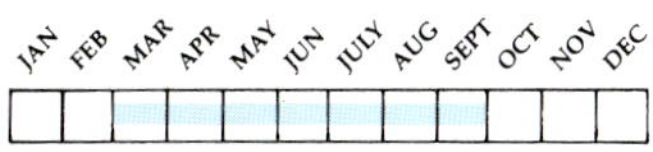

COMMON FORGET-ME-NOT

Myosotis arvensis

Characteristics: The forget-me-nots can be a confusingly similar group of plants. Like the umbellifers, a close look at certain key parts can soon tell them apart. Common Forget-me-not is an erect, hairy annual up to 30cm with a rosette of strap-shaped leaves at the base and alternate stemless leaves up the main stem. The flowers are borne on a series of spikes at the top of the plant. The pale blue flowers are up to 5mm wide, slightly cup-shaped with the corolla tube shorter than the calyx, which under a lens can be seen to be covered in hook-tipped bristles.

Range and habitat: Found throughout the British Isles except areas of northern Scotland. Widely distributed throughout Europe. A common plant of a range of well-drained soils on waste ground, fields and woodland.

Similar species: Wood Forget-me-not, *M. sylvatica*, is frequently cultivated in gardens but is also a local plant of damp woodlands. It has larger (6-10mm across), flatter flowers; the style is longer than the calyx tube.

HEDGE BINDWEED

Calystegia sepium

Characteristics: A persistent climbing perennial with large summer-flowering blooms. The plant can climb up to 3m, twisting anti-clockwise on fencing wire, hedgerow shrubs and tree branches. The leaves are large (up to 15cm) and broadly heart- or arrow-shaped. The flowers are carried singly on long stalks, usually white or pink and trumpet-shaped, up to 4cm across. Two large leaf-like bracts under the flower partially hide the calyx.

Range and habitat: Widespread and common in the British Isles except the north of Scotland; common throughout Europe. A plant of scrub, fen, woodland edges, as well as hedgerows and gardens.

Similar species: The subspecies *C. s. sylvatica*, Large Bindweed, is a naturalized plant from southern Europe which is sometimes abundant in suburban areas in south-east England. It has larger flowers (6-7.5cm) and larger inflated bracts. Field Bindweed, *Convolvulus arvensis*, is a creeping plant with usually pink and white flowers (up to 3cm across).

BITTERSWEET

Solanum dulcamara

Characteristics: A woody perennial that climbs over other plants, growing up to 2m long. The alternate leaves are oval shaped, up to 8cm with pointed tips and often with a pair of spreading leaflets at the base. The flowers are in loose branched clusters. The flower has 5, pointed, purple lobes that curl back as the flower matures. The bright yellow stamens form a narrow cone. The fruit is an oval berry which turns from green through yellow to red. A poisonous plant.

Range and habitat: Common in Britain, except for parts of Wales, north to central Scotland; it is rare or absent further north. Infrequent or absent in Ireland; common throughout Europe. A plant of scrub, woodland edges and hedges; also found in fens and beaches.

Similar species: The berries can be confused with those of Black and White Bryony but leaves are different.

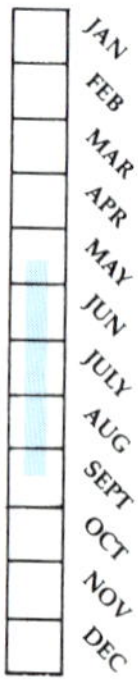

COMMON FIGWORT

Scrophularia nodosa

Characteristics: An upright perennial reaching 150cm in height, with a solid, square stem. The leaves are in opposite pairs, oval-shaped with a pointed tip and toothed. The flowers are carried in a leafy, upright branching clusters at the top of the stem. The flowers, which are pollinated by wasps, are small (up to 1cm) with a lobed calyx. They are green and globular with an open 'mouth', the reddish-brown upper lip longer than the lower one.

Range and habitat: Found throughout the British Isles except for the north of Scotland, commonest in the south of England. Widespread in Europe. A plant of damp woodland rides and edges and other shaded habitats such as hedgebanks.

Similar species: Water Figwort, *S. aquatica,* is a larger and more robust-looking plant than Common Figwort, with winged, 4-angled stems. The leaves often have a pair of leaflets at the base. It is a plant of streamsides and ponds.

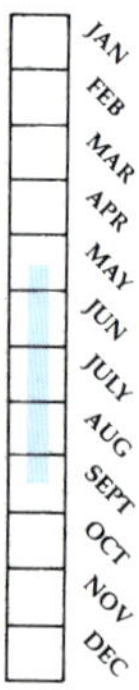

detail of flower

FOXGLOVE
Digitalis purpurea

Characteristics: A tall (up to 150cm), upright, unbranched biennial. The lower leaves form a dense rosette of wide, lanceolate, downy, greyish-green leaves, up to 30cm long. The alternate stem leaves are more obviously stalked. The flowers are in a long, tapering, many-flowered (up to 80) spike. The purple flowers are tubular to bell-shaped with dark spots on a lighter inside. The calyx-tube is 3-4 times shorter than the corolla. It is pollinated by bumble bees. Poisonous.

Range and habitat: It is found throughout the British Isles except Shetland but is scarce in the east Midlands. It is common in western Europe. Foxglove is a plant of woodland rides and clearings, heaths and hedgebanks on well-drained acid soils.

Similar species: The mulleins have a similar habit but have yellow flowers. On the Continent there is the Small Yellow Foxglove, *D. lutea*, but this is hairless and has yellow flowers.

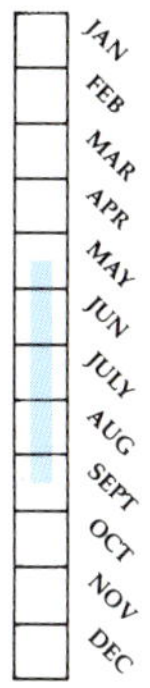

GERMANDER SPEEDWELL
Veronica chamaedrys

Characteristics: A creeping perennial with upright flowering stems. The stems have 2 opposite lines of white hairs along them. The opposite pairs of leaves have very short or no apparent stalks and are oval to heart-shaped with coarse teeth. The flowering spike arises from the leaf axils and is unbranched with flowers loosely spaced along the spike. The 5-lobed azure blue flower (1cm across) has a noticeable stalk and a distinct white eye-ring at its centre. The heart-shaped green fruits are covered in hairs and are shorter than the calyx.

Range and habitat: A common plant throughout the British Isles and Europe. It is found on well-drained soils in a wide range of habitats from grassy woodland rides, hedgebanks and scrub to grassland and waste ground.

Similar species: In woodland, could be confused with the less common Wood Speedwell, *V. montana*, but this has hairs all round the stem and clearly stalked leaves, usually a paler green.

COMMON COW-WHEAT

Melampyrum pratense

Characteristics: A semi-parasitic somewhat erect annual, up to 60cm tall. The lower leaves are lanceolate and more or less unstalked. The upper leaves can be more oval in shape. The flowers are carried in pairs both facing the same direction and arising from the slightly toothed, leaf-like bracts. The flowers are a pale buttery-yellow with a tube-shaped corolla; the two lips are usually closed. It is about twice as long as the calyx, which has long, teeth-like lobes.
Range and habitat: A widespread plant in the British Isles, although scarce in East Anglia, north-east England, Scotland and Ireland. Found throughout Europe. It is a plant typically of acid woodland found growing along ride edges and hedgebanks. It can also be found in peat bogs in Scotland and occasionally calcareous soils in southern England.
Similar species: Lesser Skullcap, *Scuttellaria minor*, can look broadly similar but has pink rather than yellow flowers.

HEDGE WOUNDWORT

Stachys sylvatica

A densely hairy, upright, unbranched perennial, up to 100cm tall. It has large, broadly oval, pointed, nettle-like leaves which, when rubbed, produce a strong fetid smell. The flower spike at the top of the plant consists of a loosely-spaced series of whorls. The flowers consist of a deep purple-red corolla tube with a hooded upper lip and a 3-lobed lower lip marked with a fine white series of stripes and blotches. The calyx is hairy with long, pointed teeth. It is pollinated by bees.
Range and habitat: A common plant throughout the British Isles except the Highlands of Scotland. Found throughout Europe. It is found on rich soils on a wide range of habitats from woodland edges, hedgebanks and streamsides, to shady gardens.
Similar species: Can be confused with Marsh Woundwort, *S. palustris*, which grows in damp habitats. This plant has unstalked, narrower leaves which do not smell when crushed; the flowers are a paler rosy-pink.

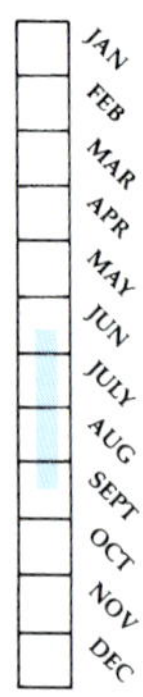

BETONY

Stachys officinalis

Characteristics: An erect perennial, up to 60cm tall. Unlike the previous species, the leaves form a rosette at the base of the plant and are oblong, with blunt teeth along the edge with a rounded tip to the leaf. The lower leaves are stalked. The stem-like leaves are widely spaced with the upper ones unstalked. The flowerhead is a compact series of whorls at the top of the plant. The flower has a reddish-purple corolla tube (15cm) with flat upper and lower lips. The calyx is about half as long as the corolla with pointed teeth.
Range and habitat: Found throughout England and Wales, though rare in East Anglia. It is very rare in Scotland and Ireland. Found in Europe north to southern Sweden. It is typically a plant of traditionally managed landscapes being found in grassland, woodland rides, commons and heaths. Usually a plant of mildly acid, lighter soils.
Similar species: The rosette of basal, blunt-toothed leaves and compact flowerhead distinguish it from other members of the *Stachys* genus.

YELLOW ARCHANGEL

Lamiastrum galeobdolon

Characteristics: An upright woodland perennial (to 60cm) with bright yellow flowers, sometimes forming extensive carpets by means of its leafy runners. The nettle-like leaves are carried in opposite pairs. The dense whorls of attractive yellow flowers are equally spaced up the stem, arising from the leaf axils. The corolla tube has 2 lips: the upper is inflated into a helmet shape, the lower is divided into 3 lobes marked with a tracery of reddish-brown lines. The calyx is much shorter than the corolla and has 5-pointed teeth. It is pollinated by bees.

Range and habitat: Found throughout England and Wales. Rare in southern Scotland and very rare in the rest of Scotland and Ireland. Found in Europe from southern Scandinavia southwards. A plant of woodland rides and hedgebanks on neutral to calcareous soils, it can be dominant in recently coppiced or cleared areas. In some areas the plant is indicative of ancient woodland, particularly if it is found with other woodland plants such as Bluebell and Sweet Woodruff.
Similar species: Superficially similar to White Dead-nettle, *Lamium album*, but, as its name suggests, this has white flowers.

GROUND IVY

Glechoma hederacea

Characteristics: A hairy, low-growing, ubiquitous perennial, the 4-sided flowering stems up to 30cm tall. The creeping stems root at intervals. The long-stalked, pungent leaves are kidney-shaped to round, with blunt teeth. The flowers are in loose whorls along the stem arising from the leaf axils. They usually face the same way. The corolla is mauve with a few darker spots on the larger central lobe of the 3-lobed lower lip. The notched upper lip is unmarked and flat. The green calyx has 5 short teeth.

Range and habitat: Found throughout the British Isles except north Scotland. Very common plant in a wide range of habitats but most typical of woodland rides and hedgebanks on heavier soils.

Similar species: Similar to other low-growing members of the labiate family but immediately recognisable by its kidney-shaped leaves.

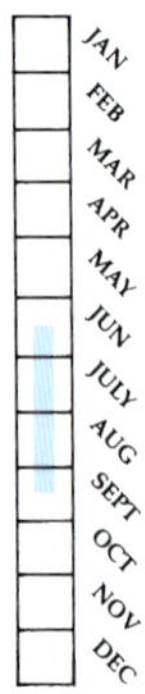

WOOD SAGE

Teucrium scorodonia

Characteristics: A downy, medium-tall (to 60cm), upright, branched perennial sometimes forming extensive patches by means of its creeping rhizomes. The leaves are held in opposite stalked pairs and are broadly heart-shaped with blunt teeth, the surface is heavily wrinkled. The flowers are borne on branched spikes near the top of the plant. The small, leaf-like bracts have no teeth. The flower has a pale yellow-green corolla with a large lower lip and no upper lip, exposing the stamens. The calyx has a large upper tooth and 4 smaller lower teeth.

Range and Habitat: A common plant throughout the British Isles; absent from Shetland and less common in East Anglia and Central Ireland. Found throughout west and central Europe, more common in the south. A plant of dry woodlands, heaths, dunes and rough grassland, usually on acidic soils.

Similar species: The only member of the labiate family with branching spikes of yellow-green flowers.

BUGLE
Ajuga reptans

Characteristics: A low-growing (up to 30cm) perennial, often forming dense mats by means of its leafy, creeping, rooting rhizomes. The square stems are hairy on opposite sides only. The basal leaves form a rosette of shiny, untoothed oblong leaves. The shorter stem leaves are unstalked, carried in opposite pairs, each pair at right angles to the next. The vivid blue (sometimes pink or mauve) flowers form a series of pagoda-like whorls at the top of the plant separated by small leaf-like bracts. The corolla has no upper lip and a lobed lower lip.
Range and habitat: Common throughout Europe and the British Isles except for northern Scotland and central Ireland. Found in damp woodland rides, hedgebanks and meadows.
Similar species: Selfheal has purple rather than blue flowers and the corolla has a hooded upper lip.

JAN FEB MAR APR MAY JUN JULY AUG SEPT OCT NOV DEC

NETTLE-LEAVED BELLFLOWER
Campanula trachelium

Characteristics: A tall, hairy, usually unbranched perennial (up to 100cm). The rough stems are sharply angled. The leaves are nettle-like and coarsely-toothed; those on the lower stem have long stalks. The flowers are in a loose, leafy panicle carrying up to 4 flowers. The purple-blue flower is 30-40mm long, bell-shaped with a lobed opening, and carried on a stalk (up to 1cm), often erect or spreading. The calyx teeth are also usually erect.
Range and habitat: In Britain found mainly in central and south-eastern England. Absent in Scotland and very rare in Ireland. Widespread and locally common in Europe. A plant of woodland rides, edges and hedgebanks on neutral to calcareous soils.
Similar species: To some extent, this species is replaced in the north by the Giant Bellflower, *C. latifolia,* which has a more rounded stem, the bases of the leaves are tapering, the teeth of the calyx are longer (up to 25mm) and the paler flower is larger (40-50mm long).

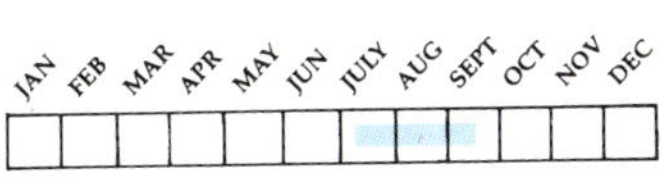

WOODRUFF

Galium odoratum

Characteristics: An upright perennial (up to 30cm) which can form dense carpets in woodland. Unlike most members of the bedstraw family, it is unbranched. The 4-angled stems have whorls of 6 to 8 lanceolate leaves with forward-pointed spines along the edge. The white flower forms a funnel-shaped corolla split into 4 blunt lobes for half its length. The fruit is covered with hooked bristles. The dried plant smells hay-scented and it was once used to cover floors and as a 'strewing herb' to hide unpleasant odours.

Range and habitat: Widely distributed in the British Isles, absent from the Scottish Islands and less common in north Scotland and Ireland. Found throughout northern and central Europe. A plant of damp, base-rich or calcareous woodlands where it can be abundant, especially after coppicing. Usually found along woodland rides and edges.

Similar species: Other white-flowered bedstraws are more branching and less erect with smaller flowers.

HEDGE BEDSTRAW

Galium mollugo

Characteristics: A weak, branching perennial (up to 100cm long) with 4-angled smooth stems. The leaves are in whorls of 6 to 8, lanceolate with forward-pointing spines on the edges. The white flowers are in a loose branching panicle, the small (c. 3mm) flowers have 4 pointed lobes. The fruits are hairless.

Range and habitat: Generally common throughout England but more scarce in Ireland, Wales and Scotland and absent in the Scottish Islands. Widespread in Europe but more common towards the south. A characteristic plant of hedgerows, scrub and woodland rides on neutral to base-rich soils.

Similar species: Some authorities recognise a very similar plant as the Upright Hedge-bedstraw, *G. album*. This is more erect with slightly larger flowers. Goosegrass or Cleavers, *G. aparine*, has strong backward-pointing spines on the stem and leaves. Hedge Bedstraw can be distinguished as it is the only white-flowered bedstraw with pointed leaf tips and a smooth stem.

fruit

HONEYSUCKLE
Lonicera periclymenum

Characteristics: A woody, twining shrub (up to 6m long) sometimes causing the branches or trunks of the supporting trees to become deformed. Also forms extensive carpets. The stems are often tinged reddish when young, becoming woody over the years. The leaves are usually oval and pointed, grey-green below. The flowers are held in a dense terminal head. The flowers consist of a long (4-5cm) corolla tube with a backward-curved, toothed, upper lip and a curved-down lower lip. The 5 stamens and style protrude well beyond the corolla. The flower is yellowish, tinged pinkish on the outside and creamy inside, darkening after pollination. The berries are red. The flower is especially aromatic in the evening. It is pollinated by hawk-moths and bumble-bees.

Range and habitat: Found throughout the British Isles and widespread in Europe. An ubiquitous plant of woodlands, hedgerows and scrub on a wide range of soils.

Similar species: None.

MOSCHATEL
Adoxa moschatellina

Characteristics: A small, erect plant (up to 10cm) forming small patches in woodlands. It is the only member of this obscure family. The leaves are on long stalks from the base of the plant with twice-trifoliate leaflets, dull green above and somewhat shiny below. The blunt lobes are tipped with a minute spine. The upright flowering stem has shorter-stalked leaves. The terminal flowerhead is very distinctive, consisting of 5, yellowish-green, 5-lobed flowers, one pointing in each direction with one on top – hence its other name, Town-hall Clock. The fruits are green and droop.

Range and habitat: In the British Isles found as far north as mid-Scotland. Very rare in Ireland. Found throughout Europe. An often overlooked but intriguing plant usually of damp woodland edges and rides, old hedgebanks and mountain rocks.

Similar species: The leaves can look like Wood Anemone but are paler and fleshy.

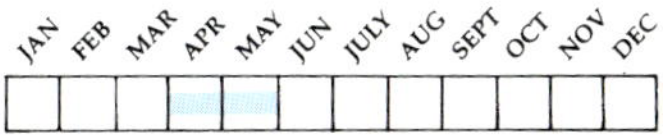

flowerhead

TEASEL

Dipsacus fullonum

Characteristics: A robust biennial. In the first year a rosette of long, pointed leaves is produced with characteristic 'warty' prickles. In the second year, a tall (up to 200cm) flowering stem grows, covered in sharp spines. Each pair of stalkless narrow leaves are fused together to form a 'cup' around the stem. The flowerheads which arise from the leaf axils in the upper part of the plant are the familiar egg-shaped mass of hundreds of pink or white flowers. They start flowering in a line along the centre of the head and work upwards and downwards. The spiny floret bracts persist through the winter. The large bracts beneath the flowerhead are narrow and spiny.
Range and habitat: Common in much of England and Wales. Rare in south-east Scotland and Ireland. Widespread in Europe. A plant especially of clay soils found along woodland rides, roadsides, waste ground and scrub.
Similar species: Small Teasel, *D. pilosus*, is a smaller local plant with a round head; stem leaves not joined.

GOLDENROD

Solidago virgaurea

Characteristics: An upright, slender perennial, up to 75cm tall. The toothed basal leaves are ovate, tapering into a short stalk. The stem leaves are narrow, pointed and more or less untoothed. The yellow flowerheads (6-10mm across), are in a loose, erect panicle, with larger outer spreading ray florets. The seeds are brown with a pappus of long white hairs.
Range and habitat: Widely distributed and common throughout most of the British Isles, more scarce in East Anglia and parts of Ireland. Widespread in Europe. Found in a wide range of habitats from mountain ledges to sand dunes. In lowland areas typically a plant of dry, sandy woods.
Similar species: Common Fleabane is a plant of damp habitats and has stem leaves that clasp the stem; the yellow flowerheads are more compact. The ragworts, which have a similar flowerhead, do not have them in an elongated panicle but more usually a loose, horizontally-branching inflorescence.

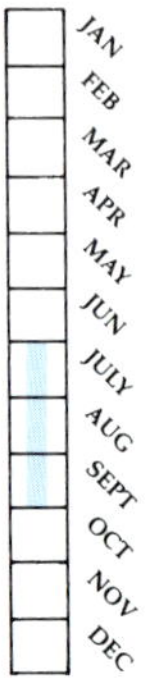

NIPPLEWORT

Lapsana communis

Characteristics: A tall (up to 90cm) annual with many ascending slender branches. The lower leaves have a very large toothed oval- or heart-shaped terminal lobe with smaller lateral lobes below and a winged stalk. The stem leaves are oval- to oblong-shaped, shortly stalked. The loose, many-branched panicle consists of 15 to 20 yellow flowerheads with paler yellow outer florets. The brown fruits do not have a pappus. The flowers close in mid-afternoon or in dull weather.

Range and habitat: Found commonly throughout the whole of the British Isles except the Scottish Highlands. Widespread and common throughout Europe. A familiar plant of hedgerows, woodland rides and glades, waste ground, walls and gardens, where it can be a nuisance.

Similar species: Told from other yellow-flowered members of the daisy family (the Compositae) by its branching habit and leafy stems, and also the lack of a crown of bristles or hairs (pappus) on the fruit.

LILY-OF-THE-VALLEY

Convallaria majalis

Characteristics: This is the same species as the common garden plant. It has a long, creeping rhizome and each spring shoots up a pair of glossy, long-stalked, broadly oval, pointed leaves, with distinct parallel veins. The nodding, one-sided spike of white flowers is up to 20cm high. The flowers are bell-shaped, with 6 teeth and are very scented. The berry is globular and red. The plant is highly poisonous.

Range and habitat: Although a common flower of gardens, the wild plant is local with a scattered distribution in England. Rare in Scotland and Wales; absent as a native plant in Ireland. Widespread in Europe. Found in dry, ash woodlands on limestone, and in woodlands on dry acid soils. Also found on limestone pavements in northern England.

Similar species: May Lily, *Maianthemum bifolium*, has a pair of pointed, heart-shaped leaves and an upright spike of open unscented flowers. In Britain it is a very rare plant of eastern England. More common in Europe.

BLUEBELL
Hyacinthoides non-scripta

Characteristics: This is the classic spring flower of British woodlands. It is a bulbous perennial growing up to 50cm tall. The long, glossy, strap-like leaves arise from the bulbous base. The leafless flowering stem is topped by a nodding, one-sided spike of long, bell-shaped flowers with curved-back teeth. Sometimes has white or pink flowers. In fruit the plant becomes more erect. After fruiting in June the plant, including the leaves, withers.
Range and Habitat: The Bluebell has the centre of its world population in Britain. It is a common, sometimes dominant, plant of woodlands on loamy, slightly acid, soils. In the east of Britain it is found in old woodlands whilst in the wetter western regions it can be found commonly in hedgerows and hillsides. Also found in the Low Countries and northern France
Similar species: The Spanish Bluebell, *H. hispanicus*, a native of south-west Europe, is a frequent garden escape. It has wider leaves and a more erect, less one-sided, paler flowering spike.

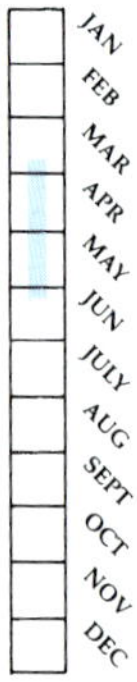

RAMSONS
Allium ursinum

Characteristics: One of the few British plants that can be recognised some way off by its smell – a strong odour of onion. It is, in fact, a species of wild garlic and its other common name is Wood Garlic. It is a bulbous flower with broad, oval, pointed leaves arising from the bulb on long stalks (up to 20cm) that are twisted through 180°. The flower stalk (up to 45cm) has 2 thin translucent bracts, shorter than the umbel-like flowerhead of stalked white star-like flowers. Unlike many members of the garlic tribe, it has no bubils.
Range and habitat: Found throughout the British Isles, although scarce or absent in parts of north Scotland and Ireland. Common in Europe north to southern Scandinavia. A plant of damp woodlands on basic loamy soils, its carpets of white flowers sometimes marking out streamsides or damper areas amidst a sea of Bluebells in woodlands in May. The flowers and leaves wither after fruiting.
Similar species: The only wild garlic with broad leaves.

WILD DAFFODIL

Narcissus pseudonarcissus

Characteristics: The daffodil is one of the most popular of our spring flowers and many varieties are available for the gardener. The Wild Daffodil is a local plant of woodlands and every bit as attractive as the garden varieties. It is a bulbous perennial with grey-green strap-like leaves arising from the underground bulb. The tall flower stalk (up to 35cm) has a solitary horizontally-held flower. The outer ring of petals or perianth segments are pale yellow with a deeper yellow, tube-like corona.

Range and habitat: Locally common throughout England; most abundant in the west and south. Rare in Wales and absent in Scotland and Ireland. A local plant of western Europe from Belgium south to Portugal. It is found in old woodlands and grasslands with damp, neutral to slightly acid soils.

Similar species: Told from many of the garden hybrids by the inner corona being darker than the outer petals. The most common garden varieties are usually larger than the Wild Daffodil.

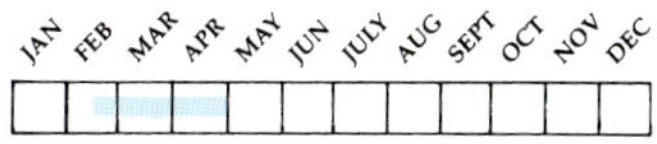

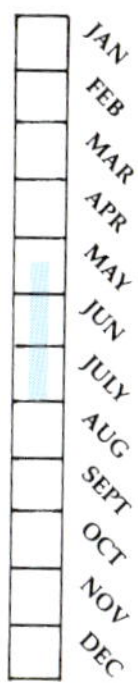

BLACK BRYONY

Tamus communis

Characteristics: A climbing perennial which gets its name from the large black underground tubers. It is our only member of the tropical yam family (Dioscoraceae). The unbranched stems (up to 4m) which arise annually, twine clockwise around shrubs and low branches of hedgerow trees. It has distinctive long-stalked, pointed, heart-shaped leaves which are a glossy green with a noticeable network of veins on the surface. The plant is dioecious with the male flowers on stalks on a long spike and the female ones more or less without a stalk. Each has 6, green-white petals. The poisonous berries are green at first, turning bright red.

Range and habitat: Found widely in England and Wales north to the North Pennines. Absent from Scotland and Ireland. Found in south and west Europe as far north as Belgium. A common plant of hedgerows, scrub and woodland edges on moist rich soils.

Similar species: White Bryony has similar red berries but has dull green palmately-lobed leaves and tendrils.

TWAYBLADE

Listera ovata

Characteristics: One of the most widespread and common of the woodland orchids, but sometimes difficult to find because of its almost uniform green colour. It is an erect perennial growing up to 60cm with a pair of distinctive, broad, ovate, green leaves (hence the name 'twayblade' or 'two-leaved'), with 3 to 5 clear parallel ribs. They are held at 45° to the stem and arise above the ground level. The flowers are in a long spike at the top of the stem and consist of small, yellow-green flowers with a hood of oval petals and a long paler lip which is split in two just over halfway down.
Range and habitat: Found throughout the British Isles except for parts of the north of Scotland. Widespread in Europe. A plant of woodland rides and glades, old pastures and hedgebanks, particularly on moist, base-rich soils.
Similar species: Told from other orchids by its pair of oval-shaped leaves. In the north there is the rarer Lesser Twayblade, *L. cordata,* but this is much smaller with a reddish stem.

EARLY PURPLE ORCHID

Orchis mascula

Characteristics: An erect perennial arising from egg-shaped underground tubers. The leaves form a rosette around the base of the plant and are lance-shaped with dark purple-brown blotches arranged lengthwise. The flowering stem is up to 60cm tall, with the flowers arranged in a loose spike in the top half. The purple flower has two erect sepals at the back with two others joining loosely with two of the petals to form a 'hood'. The lower petal is larger and hangs down to form a notched three-lobed lip with a lighter central area marked with darker purple blotches. A blunt-tipped spur protrudes from the back of the flower.
Range and habitat: Found throughout the British Isles; it is more common towards the south. Found throughout Europe. Most often found in old woods with neutral to base-rich soils, also in old hedgebanks and scrub.
Similar species: The leaves could be confused with the Common Spotted Orchid, *Dactylorhiza fuchsii.*

LORDS AND LADIES

Arum maculatum

Characteristics: A highly distinctive plant with an unusual flower structure. It is an erect, early-flowering annual, with large, long-stalked, arrow-shaped glossy leaves with a prominent network of veins, often dark spotted. The long-stalked flowerhead or spadix is enclosed in a large funnel or cowl-shaped spathe. A sterile, purplish head projects from the base of the spathe. Beneath this is a ring of hairs, followed by the male flowers, below which are the female flowers. The plant is pollinated by small midges that become trapped in the spathe, attracted by the decaying smell of the plant. The spathe withers after pollination and bright red poisonous berries later develop.
Range and habitat: Throughout the British Isles south of central Scotland. Widespread in Europe from southern Scandinavia. Found in hedgerows, scrub and gardens on base-rich soils.
Similar species: The rarer, more southern Large Lords and Ladies, *A. italicum*, has a yellow spadix and unspotted yellow-veined leaves.

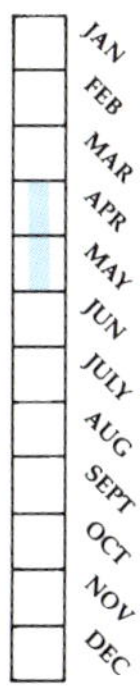

SNOWDROP

Galanthus nivalis

Characteristics: A low-growing bulbous plant which has been popular with gardeners for centuries. It has grey-green, erect, strap-like leaves. The drooping flowers are held singly on a flower stalk as tall as the leaves (up to 25cm). The delicate white flower consists of 3 outer sepals and 3 inner notched petals tipped with green.
Range and habitat: Found throughout Britain as far north as the Scottish Highlands. Absent from Ireland. This courageous little plant has been so widely planted and naturalizes so easily that there is some doubt as to its status as a native plant. The distribution on the Continent is also similarly obscured; it is native in the south. It is a plant of streamsides and damp woodland edges.
Similar species: The later flowering Summer Snowflake, *Leucojum aestivum*, is taller (to 60cm) with up to 7 flowers in a short cluster. A rare plant found only in the Thames valley in Britain.

PASTURES AND MEADOWS

Traditionally, the open countryside was made up of an intricate patchwork of fields of varying sizes, supporting a wide range of wild flowers, each field differing in its precise communities according to the aspect and drainage, as well as the soil type and management. Today, the increasing mechanisation of farming and increased arable crops has meant that, over large areas of countryside, uniform modern grass fields with perhaps a few high-yielding rye grasses alternate with fields of crops. This leaves little room for wild flowers, which hang on as relic populations on field edges and roadsides.

Fortunately, there are areas where flower-rich pastures can still be found. Look for them in poorly-drained valleys or along hillsides where tractors have difficulty gaining access. They can be spotted from afar, as even when they are not in flower the tawny lines of the various grasses and seedheads will contrast with the bright green of the heavily-fertilised modern pastures.

Traditional meadows, which are cut for hay in the summer and often grazed during the rest of the year, can harbour an enormous number of plants, including Ox-eye Daisy, Meadow Vetchling, Red Clover and Yellow Rattle. On damper meadows, plants such as Lady's Smock, Great Burnet and Devil's-bit Scabious might be found. In upland areas, look out for Globe Flower and Wood Crane's-bill.

Pastures are simply grazed areas and those that have escaped the effects of herbicides and fertilizers can be immensely rich. For example, on some chalk and limestone pastures botanists have found over 40 species of plant growing in plots of less than a square metre. Often the plants that do well are those that can stand grazing and thrive in open situations, such as Wild Thyme, Stemless Thistle and Bird's-foot Trefoil. In early summer, it is worth looking out for orchids in traditionally-managed pastures – the Common Spotted Orchid is always pleasant to find and in some districts is still common. Acid grasslands have their own particular plants, such as Tormentil and Heath Speedwell.

Cowslips and Daises in spring on a limestone hillside.

GLOBE FLOWER

Trollius europaeus

Characteristics: A tall (up to 60cm) perennial member of the buttercup family. The leaves are rather like those of Meadow Buttercup, deeply lobed, glossy green above and paler below; basal leaves are stalked, stem leaves are unstalked. The distinctive flowers are usually held singly and consist of many yellow, concave, petal-like sepals which enclose smaller petals forming a noticeable globe shape to the overall flower; 2.5-3cm across.

Range and habitat: An upland species with a distinctly northern distribution. In Britain found chiefly from Derbyshire and Wales northwards; rare in northern Ireland. Widely scattered in Europe, more common towards the north. A classic plant of lush northern pastures and hay meadows, also damp upland woodlands, streamsides and fens. In Britain it has been found in mountains as high as 1,130m.

Similar species: Told from other buttercups by its large round flowers and from Marsh Marigold by the leaf shape and deeply concave sepals.

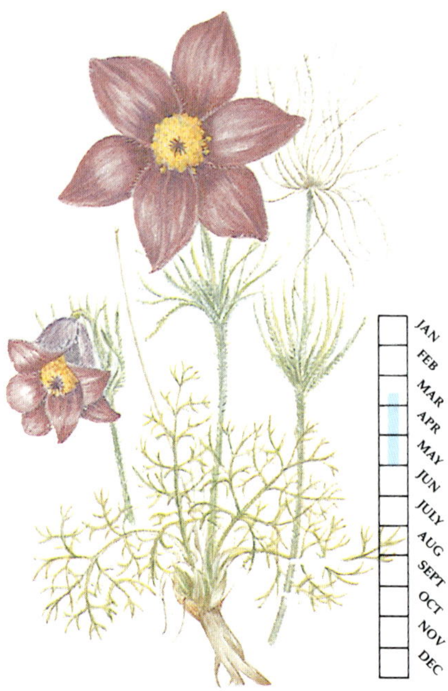

PASQUE FLOWER

Pulsatilla vulgaris

Characteristics: A beautiful but rare and declining plant of limestone grassland. It is a low-growing (up to 30cm) perennial with all parts covered in a velvety mass of silky white hairs. The rosette of leaves are finely divided, rather like a mayweed, and can be easily overlooked. The flowers are erect and open at first, later closing and nodding downwards. The bell-shaped flower consists of 6, rich-purple, petal-like sepals with a mass of golden-yellow anthers at the centre. The bracts are finely dissected and silky. In fruit, the stem elongates and becomes erect. The persistent cluster of seeds have long silky hairs, somewhat similar to the near relative, Travellers Joy.

Range and habitat: A very local species in Britain found only on limestone pastures between the Cotswolds and Lincolnshire. Ploughing and destruction of old, traditionally-managed grassland slopes has meant it is now found in only 30 sites. Widespread but local and also declining in Europe.

Similar species: None.

LESSER CELANDINE
Ranunculus ficaria

Characteristics: This delightful little flower is one of the heralds of the spring flowering season with its golden-yellow flowers that splash hedgerows and field edges with colour from early March onwards. It is a low-growing, creeping perennial, up to 25cm tall, often forming extensive carpets of flowers in the right conditions. The stalked leaves are heart-shaped and glossy, forming a rosette. The flowers are on the end of a long stem with 3 green sepals and 8 to 12 glossy, yellow, strap-shaped petals.
Range and habitat: Found commonly throughout the British Isles. Widespread and common in Europe. A sometimes abundant plant of damp grassy banks, streamsides and woodland edges.
Similar species: Told from 'buttercups' by the heart-shaped leaves and flower with three sepals and many narrow petals.

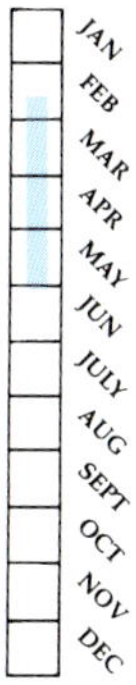

MEADOW BUTTERCUP
Ranunculus acris

Characteristics: There are three common grassland species of buttercup. The tallest (up to 100cm) is the Meadow Buttercup, which has long-stalked, deeply-dissected leaves, the lobes radiating out from the tip of the stalk. The flowering stem is not ribbed. The green sepals under the 5-petalled yellow flower usually clasp the petals.
Range and habitat: A very common species throughout the British Isles and Europe. A classic meadow plant.
Similar species: The slightly earlier flowering Bulbous Buttercup, *R. bulbosus*, can be differentiated by its combination of reflexed sepals and a ribbed flowering stem; the terminal lobe of the leaf has a short stalk and the base of the plant is noticeably swollen into a bulb-like structure. It is typical of well-drained, basic soils. The Creeping Buttercup, *R. repens*, has rooting runners and can be an invasive garden weed. It can be told by this habit and the combination of a ribbed stem, clasping sepals and stalked leaflets. It is most often found on heavy, damp soils.

Creeping Buttercup

Bulbous Buttercup

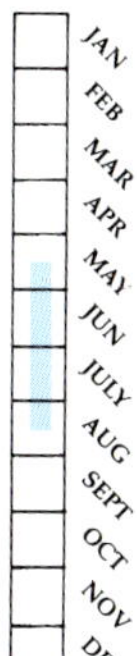

Meadow Buttercup

CUCKOO FLOWER

Cardimine pratense

Characteristics: This attractive flower is also known as Lady's Smock. It is an upright (up to 60cm) perennial with pinnate, watercress-like leaves forming a rosette; the stem leaves are smaller and narrower. The large, open, 4-petalled flower (up to 18mm across) varies in colour from lilac to pale pink or sometimes white. The anthers are yellow. The seed pod (up to 40mm) is held erect. Cuckoo Flower is the food plant of the Orange Tip caterpillar and in May it is often possible to find the bright orange egg of the butterfly beneath the flower buds.

Range and habitat: A widespread and common plant throughout the British Isles and Europe. A plant of damp meadows and marshes, streamsides and damp woodland rides.

Similar species: Large Bitter-cress, *C. amara*, can have similar-sized flowers but they are usually white, and the anthers are violet. It is a plant of wet flushes in woodland.

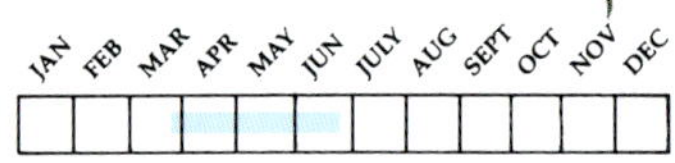

COMMON ROCK-ROSE

Helianthemum nummularium

Characteristics: A low (up to 30cm tall), creeping, partly evergreen perennial with branching stems arising from a woody base. The opposite pairs of leaves are narrow, oval-shaped, bright green above, felted and grey-green below. The flowers (up to 2.5mm across) are carried in a loose spike, with 5, golden-yellow, crinkled petals, drooping in bud. In wet weather and overcast conditions it closes its petals.

Range and habitat: Widespread throughout Britain but absent from Cornwall, the Isle of Man and areas of north-west Scotland. Found in only one place in Ireland. Widespread in Europe. A classic plant of limestone and chalk grassland through most of its range, particularly in short turf. Also found among chalky hedgebanks and scrub. In north-east Scotland, it can be found growing in dry, acid grassland.

Similar species: Two very rare species of rock-rose can be found growing on western carboniferous limestone rocks in a few localities.

COMMON ST JOHN'S-WORT

Hypericum perforatum

Characteristics: An upright, hairless perennial growing up to 90cm tall. The stems are round with 2 distinct ridges on opposite sides with blunt, oblong pairs of stalkless leaves covered in tiny translucent dots. The open, 5-petalled flowers are golden-yellow with black dots along the edges. The 5 sepals are pointed.

Range and habitat: Widespread and common throughout most of the British Isles; rarer in Scotland. A plant of commons, woodland rides, rough pasture and hedgebanks on neutral to basic soils.

Similar species: There are several similar-looking St John's-worts. Square-stemmed St John's-wort, *H. tetrapterum*, has a square, 4-winged stem and is found in damper grassland. The more local Imperforate St John's-wort, *H. maculatum*, has a square, un-winged stem and blunt sepals. Hairy St John's-wort, *H. hirsutum*, has a round stem and is hairy with pale yellow flowers and stalked black dots along the sepal edges. A plant of scrub on basic soils.

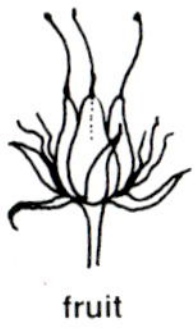

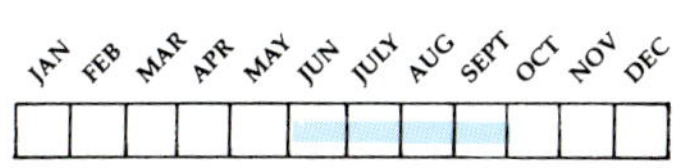

SLENDER ST JOHN'S-WORT

Hypericum pulchrum

Characteristics: A slender, erect hairless perennial, growing up to 50cm tall. An attractive rather elegant plant which has been described as one of the loveliest of wild flowers. Its stem is round and reddish with pairs of blunt-tipped leaves, heart-shaped at the base, clasping the stem; covered in translucent perforations. The flowers are up to 15mm across, in terminal clusters and have reddish buds and golden yellow petals typically dotted with red. The sepals are blunt tipped and the edges have black dots. The name St John's-wort comes from an association with the Knights of St John who used members of this family to heal wounds during the Crusades. The tiny, translucent glands were supposed to resemble wounds and therefore according to the medieval 'doctrine of signatures', which assumed that there was a link between the appearance of the plant and its ability to cure the part of the body that was diseased or injured, was widely used for battle injuries.

Range and habitat: Widespread throughout the British Isles and Europe. A plant of rough grassland, heaths and woodland rides on dry, acid soils.

Similar species: Told from other St John's-worts by the slender erect habit, round stems and heart-shaped leaves.

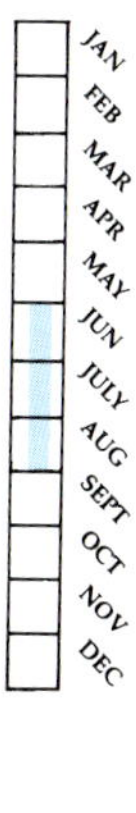

COMMON MILKWORT

Polygala vulgaris

Characteristics: A low-growing attractive perennial. A branching plant, woody at the base, with erect stems up to 10cm. The narrow, oval-shaped leaves are loosely alternate along the stem, with a short, open spike of flowers at the top. The tiny flowers have a complicated structure with tiny green outer sepals and large, blue, petal-like, pointed inner sepals. The petals form a blue frilled tube in the centre. The colour of the flower is variable and pink and white forms are not uncommon.

Range and habitat: Widespread in the British Isles and Europe. Commonly found amongst short, well-drained turf on a wide range of soils from chalk downs to heathlands.

Similar species: The Heath Milkwort, *P. serpyllifolia*, is very similar but has opposite lower leaves, slightly smaller, deeper-coloured flowers and is restricted to acid soils. Chalk Milkwort, *P. calcarea*, has brighter blue flowers; the larger lower leaves form a rosette; local, on chalk and limestone only.

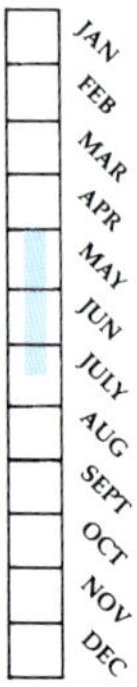

RAGGED ROBIN

Lychnis flos-cuculi

Characteristics: An upright, slender perennial up to 75 cm tall. The leaves are in opposite pairs up the stem, stalkless; they are narrow with a pointed tip and hairless but rough to touch. The upper leaves are smaller and narrower, clasping the stem. The distinctive 'ragged' flower consists of 5 rose-red petals each divided into 4 strap-like lobes. The reddish-green calyx tube has strong veins and 5 short teeth. The 'robin' in the name is probably the evil goblin, Robin Goodfellow, making it bad luck to pick the plant.

Range and habitat: A locally common and widespread plant throughout the British Isles and Europe. It is a characteristic plant of marshes, fens, riversides and damp meadows and wet woodland rides.

Similar species: The whole plant has the appearance of a slender 'ragged' version of Red Campion but that plant is a densely hairy plant with notched rather than strap-like petals.

LESSER STITCHWORT
Stellaria graminea

Characteristics: A common perennial with smooth, weak stems producing many flowering and non-flowering, semi-erect, leafy shoots (up to 90cm long). The opposite pairs of leaves are pointed, strap-shaped, clasping the stem, with smooth edges. The flowers are held in a loose, branching head. The white flowers are up to 12mm across with 5 deeply-divided petals (split more than halfway), equalling or longer than the narrow, pointed green sepals.

Range and habitat: Widespread and common; found throughout the British Isles and Europe. It is found in a wide range of grassy habitats from rough pastures and commons to hedgebanks, usually on neutral to acid soils.

Similar species: More slender and smaller than Greater Stitchwort which is a species of damper, more shaded habitats; also flowers later. Bog Stitchwort, *S. alsine*, is even smaller with tiny star-like flowers, the petals of which are shorter than the pointed sepals. Chickweed has broader leaves.

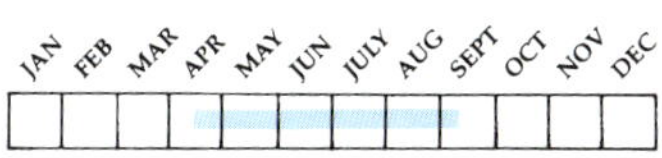

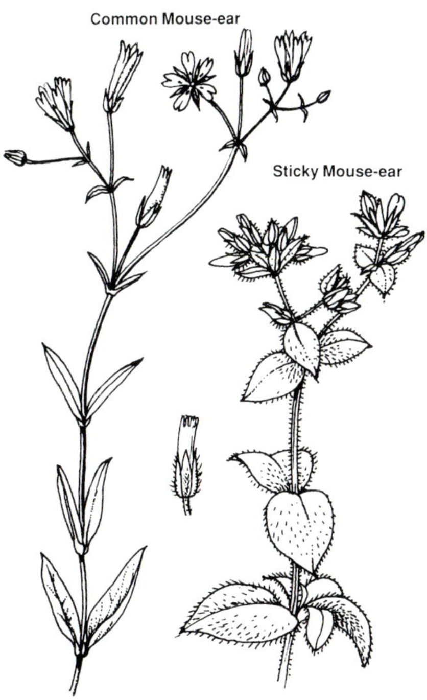

COMMON MOUSE-EAR
Cerastium fontanum

Characteristics: A densely hairy, low-growing perennial with non-flowering and flowering shoots up to 45cm (usually below 20cm). Leaves in opposite pairs, narrow and usually blunt and stalkless. Flowers in a loose, branching spike with leaf-like bracts. The white petals are notched and usually the same length as the sepals, which have papery edges; flower 12-25cm across.

Range and habitat: A widespread plant found throughout the British Isles and Europe. A common, sometimes abundant, plant of a wide range of habitats, usually on neutral to basic soils. Found in rough grassland, hedgebanks, roadsides, woodlands, shingle, dunes and mountain scree.

Similar species: The most common of the mouse-ear species, many of which are rare or local. Sticky Mouse-ear, *C. glomeratum*, can be common on sandy soils but has no glandular hairs and a dense head of flowers. Mouse-ears can be told from the stitchworts by having 5 rather than 3 styles.

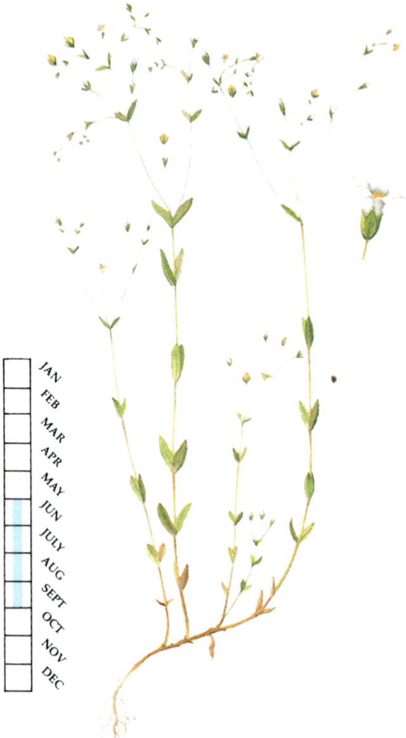

FAIRY FLAX

Linum catharticum

Characteristics: A slender, erect, hairless annual up to 25cm tall. Leaves strap-shaped and blunt-tipped, unstalked in opposite pairs widely spaced along the stem. The widely-branching head of flowers has tiny (4-6mm), pure white, star-like flowers with 5, narrow, unnotched petals. It has globular fruits. Despite its delicate appearance, Fairy Flax was used by medieval herbalists as a strong purgative, hence its other name of Purging Flax.

Range and habitat: Widespread throughout the British Isles and northern and central Europe. A common and typical plant of calcareous grassland, scree, fens, dunes and, less commonly, heathland.

Similar species: Its small, white flowers gives it the appearance of a sandwort, but the sepals are much shorter than the petals. The other flaxes have larger, pale blue flowers.

DOVE'S-FOOT CRANE'S-BILL

Geranium molle

Characteristics: A common branching annual, up to 40cm, usually shorter. Most parts of the plant are softly hairy. The lower leaves are broadly circular in outline and have dissected lobes for about two-thirds of the width. The stem leaves are shorter-stalked and smaller. The small flowers (15mm across) have deep pink, notched petals and hairy sepals. The fruit has the distinctive 'crane's-bill' of the family. The name refers to the felt-like hairiness of the lobed leaves.

Range and habitat: Widespread throughout the British Isles, except parts of northern Scotland. A common plant of dry grassland, roadside verges, field verges and waste ground on a wide range of soil types.

Similar species: There are several similar species of crane's-bill of which this species is the commonest. It is easily confused with the Small-flowered Crane's-bill, *G. pusillum*, but *G. molle* has longer hairs and hairless fruits. All 10 stamens have anthers, whereas in *G. pusillum* only 5 have anthers.

MEADOW CRANE'S-BILL

Geranium pratense

Characteristics: A distinctive, upright, densely hairy perennial up to 80cm tall. The Meadow Buttercup-like basal leaves are borne on long stalks and have 5 to 7 deep lobes which in turn are lobed, the tips of which are pointed; overall leaf blade up to 15cm across. Stem leaves are smaller with shorter stalks. The flowers are held in pairs on drooping stalks and are large (up to 18mm across) with 5, striking, violet-blue, unnotched petals, with lighter veins.
Range and habitat: Found throughout most of the British Isles. Absent from parts of the south-west of England, northern Scotland and most of southern Ireland. A plant of field edges, hedgebanks and meadows, mainly on neutral to basic soils.
Similar species: There are several hedgerow and field-edge crane's-bills that might be confused, but all have more restricted distributions. Bloody Crane's-bill, *G. sanguineum*, is found in the north and west on calcareous soils and has solitary, deep red flowers.

RESTHARROW

Ononis repens

Characteristics: A low, creeping, woody perennial up to 60cm long, covered in hairs. Usually without spines. The leaves (up to 20mm) are usually trifoliate (three-leaflets), sometimes they have just the terminal leaflet. Leaflets oval, toothed and blunt-tipped, with a toothed, lighter green stipule clasping the stem. The pea-like flowers are pink; the pod is held erect. The plant is named after the underground stems which are supposed to be so tough they could stop a horse-drawn plough.
Range and habitat: Widespread in Britain north to central Scotland. Rare in Ireland. Found in western and central Europe. A plant of rough grassland, field edges and hedgebanks, on basic soils. In the western part of its range, most commonly found near the coast.
Similar species: The Spiny Restharrow, *O. spinosa*, has a more erect habit, noticeable spines and two lines of hairs along the stem. It is more restricted in its range and is rare or absent in western and northern Britain.

RED CLOVER

Trifolium pratense

Characteristics: An abundant low-growing, downy perennial; the most commonly found clover. It grows up to 60cm tall with long-stalked, trifoliate leaves; the oval-shaped leaflets usually have a white 'chevron' mark across the middle. The stipules are sharply pointed and veined. The egg-shaped or spherical flowerheads are usually stalkless and are various shades of pinkish-purple. The plant is widely cultivated for its nitrogen-fixing properties. The petals of the flowerhead persist in fruit.

Range and habitat: Found throughout the British Isles and Europe. It is found commonly in a wide range of grassy habitats, from garden lawns and roadsides to rough pasture and chalk downland.

Similar species: The Zigzag Clover, *T. medium*, is a more local species with narrower, darker leaves, usually without the 'chevron' mark. The flowerhead is darker and stalked.

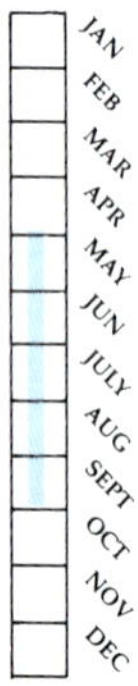

WHITE CLOVER

Trifolium repens

Characteristics: A low, creeping, hairless perennial, rooting at the nodes. The trifoliate leaves have long stalks; the leaflets are oval and shallowly toothed, usually with a white crescent mark across the bottom half. The white, sometimes pink, flowerheads are also on long stalks arising from the creeping stems, and are spherical in shape. Like Red Clover, the petals persist in fruit. It is pollinated by bees. Also known as Dutch Clover.

Range and habitat: A widespread and sometimes abundant plant throughout Britain and Europe. It is widely planted as a fodder crop and can be found in most grassy places. In garden lawns its rooting stems mean that it can be a troublesome weed.

Similar species: Alsike Clover, *T. hybridum*, looks similar but it does not have the creeping stems or the white leaflet markings, and the flowers at the base of the flowerhead often have a pinkish tinge. A plant of grassland and waste ground, formerly a fodder crop.

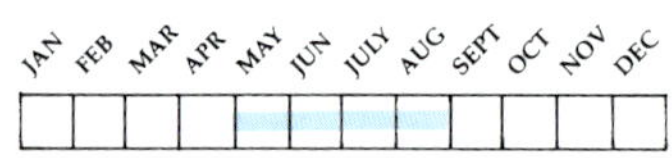

BLACK MEDICK
Medicago lupulina

Characteristics: A low-growing, downy annual with erect stems (usually to 25cm); the trifoliate leaves are long-stalked and the leaflets are oval, blunt-ended and minutely toothed, with a tiny spike at the tip. The stalked, yellow flowerhead is compact (3-8mm) and the kidney-shaped pods are black and coiled; unlike the clovers, the petals do not persist. Together with the next species, it has been sold as 'Shamrock'.
Range and habitat: Found throughout the British Isles, but more coastal in its distribution in Scotland. It is widespread in Europe. It is typically a plant of base-rich pasture but can also be found on lawns and roadsides.
Similar species: Trefoils are very similar (see below).

LESSER TREFOIL
Trifolium dubium

Characteristics: A low-growing, more-or-less hairless annual with ascending shoots to 25cm. The leaves are broadly oval and wider above the middle, sometimes notched at the tip but without the central spine of Black Medick. The flowerhead is less compact than the other trefoils, with usually between 10 and 20 yellow flowers which turn brown and hide the pods.
Range and habitat: A widespread plant found through the British Isles except in the Scottish mountains. A typical species of short-grazed turf on well-drained soils.
Similar species: Can easily be confused with the other two species on this page.

HOP TREFOIL
Trifolium campestre

Characteristics: A slightly larger, more erect annual than Lesser Trefoil, up to 35cm tall. It is also more hairy. The terminal leaflet has a longer stalk and the flowerhead is more dense with usually between 20 and 40 yellow flowers. In fruit these turn brown and hang downwards like a minute hop flowerhead, hence the name.
Range and habitat: Found in similar short grassland habitat to Lesser Trefoil, but more local in the north of Scotland and Ireland.
Similar species: See the above two species.

Black Medick

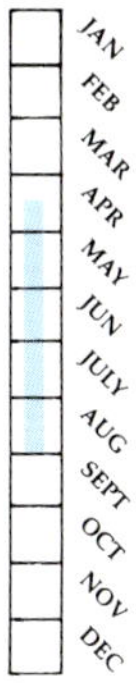

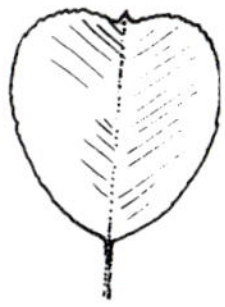
leaf

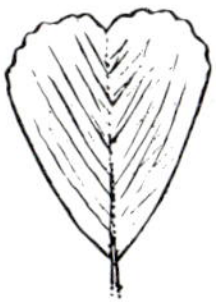
leaf

Lesser Trefoil

Hop Trefoil

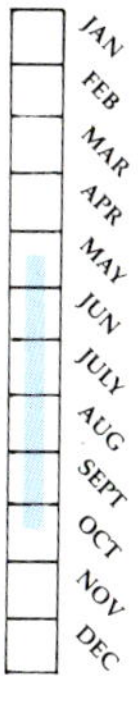

COMMON VETCH

Vicia sativa

Characteristics: A downy annual, sometimes erect but often scrambling, up to 40cm long. It has 4 to 8 pairs of leaflets with usually branched tendrils at the end of the leaf. The leaflet tips are either pointed or notched, with a tiny spine. The leaf axil has a serrated half arrow-shaped stipule, often with a black spot underneath. The bright purple-pink, pea-like flowers (up to 30mm across) arise in ones or twos from the leaf axils and are stalkless. The seed pod is up to 70mm long with 4 to 12 seeds. There are two subspecies of this plant. *V. s. sativa* is a more robust plant and was widely used as a fodder crop; the native, *V. s. angustifolia*, is smaller with pods usually between 20-30cm long and no constrictions between the seeds.

Range and habitat: Widely distributed in Britain and Europe. A plant of grassy places, such as hedgebanks and pasture, usually on neutral to basic soils.

Similar species: Bush Vetch, *V. sepium*, has groups of between 2 to 6 flowers on short stems and broader leaflets.

HAIRY TARE

Vicia hirsuta

Characteristics: A hairless (except for the pods), slender annual, sometimes forming a three-dimensional web of stems among long grass and other plants. Its leaflets are in 4 to 8 pairs and are up to 12mm long with a tiny spine at the tip. The tendrils at the end of the leaflets are usually branched. The spike of 1 to 9 tiny flowers is held on a long stalk. The flowers are a pale lilac colour. The pods are about 10mm long, hairy and 2-seeded. At one time this plant was a despised cornfield weed as the climbing stems could smother the wheat.

Range and habitat: Widespread in the British Isles but becoming rarer to the north and west. It is now more typically a plant of rough pasture, scrub and waste ground on well-drained soils.

Similar species: Smooth Tare, *V. tetrasperma*, is similar but has a more southerly distribution, being rare in Scotland and Ireland and growing on heavier, moister soils. It has a hairless, 4-seeded pod and lilac flowers.

MEADOW VETCHLING

Lathyrus pratense

Characteristics: A clambering perennial, up to 120cm, with a square stem. The lance-shaped leaflets are in single pairs with a terminal tendril, which can be branched or simple, arising from the end of the leaf. Leaf-like arrow-shaped stipules clasp the junction of the leaf and stem. The spike of 5 to 12 yellow flowers are borne on long stalks. The flattened pod has 5 to 10 seeds and is hairless.

Range and habitat: A widespread and common plant throughout the British Isles except for areas of north Scotland. Found throughout Europe; rare in the south. It is a characteristic plant of grassy places such as rough pasture, woodland rides, roadsides and hedgebanks, on a wide range of soils.

Similar species: The only common vetchling with yellow flowers. The Bitter Vetch, *L. montanus,* has 2 to 4 pairs of leaflets and blue to blood-red flowers. It is a plant of woodland rides and hedgerows on acid soil.

COMMON BIRD'S-FOOT TREFOIL

Lotus corniculatus

Characteristics: A familiar, usually hairless, low-growing perennial, 10-40cm long. The leaves have 5, oval leaflets; the bottom leaflets appear to clasp the stem as the leaf is very short-stalked. The long-stalked flowerhead has a whorl of 2 to 6 yellow, pea-like flowers, often tinged or streaked red – hence its other name, Bacon-and-eggs.

Range and habitat: A common and widespread plant throughout the British Isles and Europe. A classic plant of short grassland, found on various soils and habitats, from heaths and roadsides to cliff-tops and chalk downs.

Similar species: Greater Bird's-foot Trefoil, *L. uliginosus,* is a more robust plant of damper places. It can be told by its hairy stems and leaves, hollow stems, and sharply down-turned teeth on the hairy calyx. The flowerhead also usually has more flowers. Narrow-leaved Bird's-foot Trefoil, *L. tenuis,* has very narrow leaflets (usually no more than 3mm). It is a southern species and mostly found near the coast.

Greater Bird's-foot Trefoil

Common Bird's-foot Trefoil

KIDNEY VETCH

Anthyllus vulneraria

Characteristics: A downy, low-growing perennial up to 60cm, often shorter. Leaves with usually 4 pairs of leaflets with terminal leaflet which in lower leaves may be much larger or the only part of the leaf present. Leaflets all the same size in upper leaves. The flowerheads are made up of many tightly clustered yellow flowers and are usually in pairs with a ruff of green leaf-like bracts below. Each flower has a swollen, woolly calyx, giving the whole head a cottony appearance. Flowers can be sometimes very varied in colour near the sea with white, red and pink forms.

Range and habitat: Widespread throughout the British Isles and Europe. A characteristic plant of dry calcareous soils inland and also thin soils near the sea.

Similar species: Horseshoe Vetch, *Hippocrepis comosa*, can be found in similar habitats but is immediately identified by its wavy pod, like a line of miniature horseshoes. It is more or less hairless.

TORMENTIL

Potentilla erecta

Characteristics: A low-growing, creeping perennial with erect flower shoots to 30cm, usually below 10cm. The basal leaves, which are palmate with 4 to 5 leaflets, wither before the plant flowers. The toothed stem leaves are unstalked, with 3 leaflets but 2 leaf-like stipules at the base which make them look like they have 5 leaflets. The leaves are silky below and glossy green above. The flower is on a long stalk and usually has 4, bright yellow, slightly notched petals.

Range and habitat: Found commonly throughout the British Isles and Europe. A plant of a wide range of grasslands but can be particularly abundant on well-drained, sandy soils.

Similar species: Creeping Cinquefoil, *P. reptans*, looks similar but does not have erect stems but long, creeping, rooting ones from which arise long-stalked leaves with 5 leaflets. The stipules are not toothed like the leaves. The flowers, also on long stalks from the creeping stems, have 5 petals. The two species sometimes hybridize.

LADY'S MANTLE

Alchemilla vulgaris agg.

Characteristics: A complex group of mostly upland plants consisting of several very similar micro-species and subspecies. These perennial plants usually have large, distinctive, palmately-lobed, pleated, toothed leaves and a stalked head of many small, yellow-green flowers with 4 sepals but no petals and 4 calyx lobes. The leaves can often be picked out amongst low vegetation by the large beads of 'dew' near their tips and veins. These are, in fact, exuded by the plant in humid conditions. This 'celestial liquid' was widely used by alchemists in the Middle Ages – hence the scientific name '*Alchemilla*', meaning 'little alchemical one'.

Range and habitat: A widespread plant found throughout the British Isles and Europe. Most frequent in upland areas. A plant of meadows and upland pastures, grassy roadside verges and rock ledges.

Similar species: This group is apomictic, that means it is self-fertile and is able to produce exactly similar offspring – a form of clone.

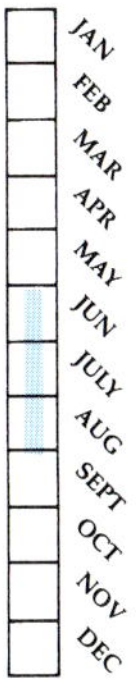

SALAD BURNET

Sanguisorba minor

Characteristics: Low-growing, more or less hairless perennial with erect flowering stems. The lower leaves form a rosette and are pinnate with up to 12 pairs of oval or round, deeply-toothed leaflets. The few stem leaves are like smaller versions of the basal leaves with narrower leaflets. The flowerhead is globular and consists of many tiny green flowers. The female flowers, with distinctive red styles, are found in the top half and the male flowers, with long yellow stamens, at the bottom. The flowers in the middle are hermaphrodite.

Range and habitat: Widespread throughout England and Wales, becoming rare in southern Scotland. Rare and local in Ireland. Widespread in central and southern Europe. It can be an abundant indicator of calcareous grassland on well-drained soils.

Similar species: Fodder Burnet, *S. m. muricata*, is a former fodder crop that has become naturalised in some places. It looks larger and more robust. See also Great Burnet.

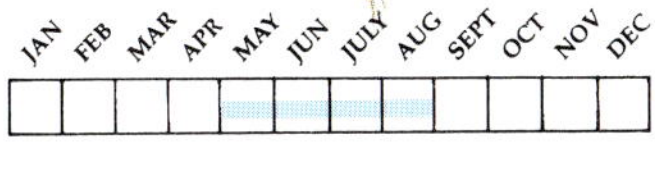

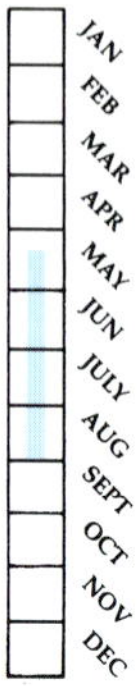

DROPWORT

Filipendula vulgaris

Characteristics: A hairless, erect perennial, usually growing up to 60cm tall. The basal leaves are up to 25cm with 8 to 20 pairs of pointed, oblong, toothed leaflets (the terminal leaflet 3-lobed), forming a loose rosette. Stem leaves few, not pinnate. The flowerhead of many white flowers is broader than it is long. The flowers have 6 white petals tinged red below, 10-20mm across. The fruit is downy and untwisted.

Range and habitat: A widespread plant with a scattered distribution in the south and west of Britain, being found only rarely in northern England, Scotland, Wales and Ireland. It is a locally abundant plant of well-drained basic soils, most typically the chalk and limestone hills of England.

Similar species: Meadowsweet, *F. ulmaria*, is a common plant of wet soils and has larger, pinnate leaves, silvery below, and a dense flowerhead of smaller, sweetly-scented flowers. The fruits are twisted, like a 'whorl of butter'. It is usually much taller.

MEADOW SAXIFRAGE

Saxifraga granulata

Characteristics: A small, erect perennial with flower stems up to 50cm (usually shorter). The axils of the basal leaves have small bubils which overwinter. These stalked, bluntly-lobed, kidney-shaped leaves form a rosette which soon withers. A few smaller, shorter-stalked leaves grow on the stem. The flowers are in a loose, branching head, each solitary on a long sticky stalk with 2 to 12 flowers. The flower has large, white petals, often curved back, and is up to 2cm across.

Range and habitat: A widespread but local plant of much of the British Isles but absent from regions of the north of Scotland and south-west England. Rare in Ireland. Widespread in Europe. A plant most typical of dry, neutral to basic grassland in the east of England but also found in river meadows and wood edges.

Similar species: Rue-leaved Saxifrage, *S. tridactylites*, is smaller, with red-tinged, lobed, strap-like leaves and tiny flowers; also a local species of dry, well-drained habitats.

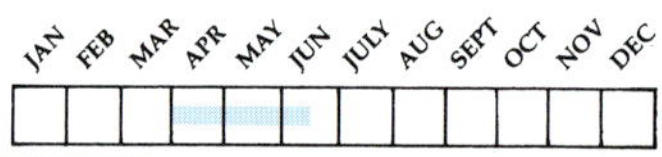

BURNET SAXIFRAGE

Pimpinella saxifraga

Characteristics: An erect, downy perennial member of the umbel or carrot family, up to 100cm tall. The stem is slightly ridged and rough. The basal leaves are pinnate with deeply-toothed oval leaflets rather like Salad Burnet or Dropwort, with which it can grow. The few stem leaves are much more finely divided and narrower. The typical white-flowered, umbel-like flowerhead has no bracts or bracteoles. The flowerhead droops in bud. The fruits are round and shiny. The plant was called a saxifrage or 'stone-breaker' as it was thought to cure gallstones.

Range and habitat: A common and widespread plant in the British Isles and Europe, although it is rare or absent in parts of northern Scotland. It is a plant of dry grassland on basic soils.

Similar species: Told immediately from most other members of the umbel family by the combination of finely-divided, pinnate leaves and absence of bracts and bracteoles on the white, flat-topped flowerhead.

PEPPER SAXIFRAGE

Silaum silaus

Characteristics: This plant is neither peppery nor a saxifrage but is a typical upright, yellow-flowered umbellifer with ridged stems up to 100cm tall. The basal leaves are 2-pinnate with narrow, pointed, strap-shaped leaflets. The flowerheads are on long stalks and have 5 to 10 rays, usually forming a broadly-domed, open cluster with no bracts but a ring of lance-shaped bracteoles. Fruit is smooth and egg-shaped.

Range and habitat: A widespread but decreasing plant found principally in central and southern England. Found less frequently as far north as Fife. Rare in Wales and absent in Ireland. In Europe found in southern and central regions. A plant of meadows and pastures on heavy clay soils; also found on hedgebanks. It is often a characteristic plant of old meadows.

Similar species: Wild Parsnip, *Pastinaca sativa,* also has yellow flowers but has much broader leaflets. Fennel, *Foeniculum vulgare,* has even narrower leaflets than Pepper Saxifrage and has no bracteoles.

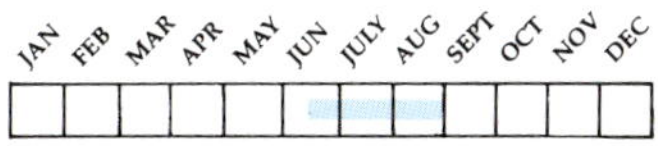

HOGWEED

Heracleum sphondylium

Characteristics: A large, biennial umbellifer, growing up to 2m tall. The hairy stems are ridge and hollow. The large (up to 60cm long) leaves are pinnate with coarsely-toothed, lobed leaflets, rough to touch. The flowerhead is a typical umbel with between 7 and 20 rays, with no bracts and narrow bracteoles. The flowers are white to pink and deeply notched; the outer flowers have petals of uneven size. The fruit is round with darker glands.

Range and habitat: Common throughout the British Isles. Widespread in Europe. This is one of the most common umbellifers and is a sometimes abundant plant of hedgebanks, roadsides, waste ground and rough pasture.

Similar species: Giant Hogweed, *H. mantegazzianum*, is like an enormous version of Hogweed, growing up to 4m. It is a garden alien from the Caucasus which is becoming increasingly naturalized along rivers and roadsides. It can cause the skin to blister in strong sunlight if touched.

WILD CARROT

Daucus carota

Characteristics: An erect, hairy, biennial umbellifer growing up to 100cm tall. It has a ridged, solid, hairy stem and fern-like, 3-pinnate leaves with strap-like leaflets. The dense flowerhead has many large, feathery, 3-pointed bracts below. The flowerhead often has a single reddish-purple flower at its centre. The fruits are round and bristly. The whole flowerhead starts off as a flat or even dome-shape. In fruit it becomes concave, forming a distinctive 'bird's-nest' appearance. This plant is the wild ancestor of the garden carrot and the leaves have the well-known 'carroty' smell.

Range and habitat: Found throughout the British Isles and Europe. Most common near the coast but also found inland, particularly in the south and east. A typical plant of grassland and roadsides on basic soils.

Similar species: The large, 3-pronged bracts distinguish it from other umbellifers.

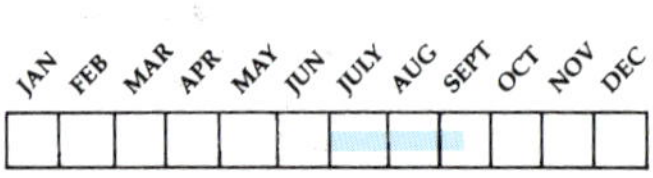

COMMON SORREL

Rumex acetosa

Characteristics: A slender, upright member of the dock family, up to 100cm tall. The leaves are long and vaguely arrow-shaped, the pointed basal lobes pointing downwards. The lower leaves are stalked; upper leaves are unstalked with the pointed basal lobes clasping the stem. The flowers are in terminal spikes at the top of the plant and consist of whorls of small greenish flowers; male and female on separate plants. The winged fruits become reddish with age. The leaves have been used for flavouring sauces for centuries.

Range and habitat: A widespread and common plant throughout the British Isles and Europe. A plant of a wide range of grasslands, from woodland rides and meadows to roadsides and shingle, on neutral to acid soils.

Similar species: Sheep's Sorrel, *R. acetosella,* is smaller than Common Sorrel with the basal lobes curling up; stem leaves stalked. Often found in sandy grassland and heaths.

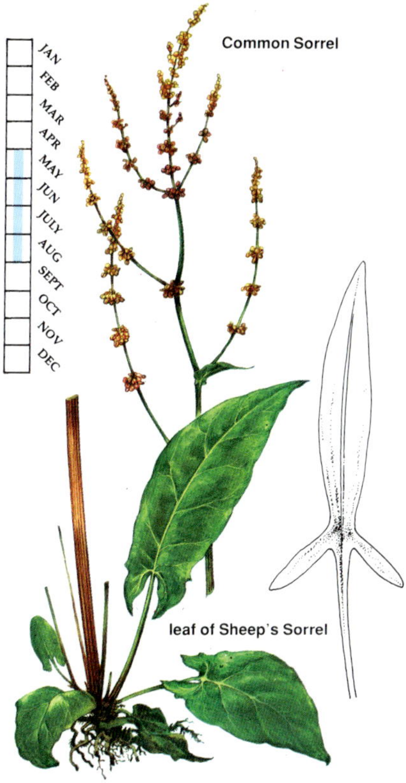

COWSLIP

Primula veris

Characteristics: A well-loved and familiar perennial growing to 30cm high. The downy, crinkled leaves arise in a rosette, the leaf blade abruptly tapering towards the base. The cluster of flowers are on the end of a long leafless stalk. The flowers are coloured deep orange-yellow, with orange streaks at the base of the lobes. The long calyx is pale-green with blunt teeth, inflated in fruit. The scented flowers have been used to make wines, but the plant is decreasing and should be left for others to enjoy.

Range and habitat: Found throughout the British Isles but rare in north-west Scotland and rare in the far west and Ireland. A classic plant of old pastures and meadows as well as undisturbed hedgebanks and woodland rides where it can hybridize with the Primrose. It is less common than it used to be.

Similar species: Oxlip, *P. elatior,* is a local species of East Anglian clay woods and central Europe. It has paler flowers all facing the same way.

COMMON CENTAURY

Centaurium erythraea

Characteristics: This attractive member of the Gentian family is a common annual. It is an erect, hairless plant up to 40cm tall, although in some conditions it can be very small. It has a rosette of oval leaves and pairs of stalkless stem leaves. The flowers are in dense clusters at the end of branching stalks. The pink flowers have 5 flat, pointed, oval lobes with yellow anthers. The long calyx tube has 5 ridged teeth.

Range and habitat: A widespread and common plant throughout England and Wales and parts of Ireland. It has a more coastal distribution in Scotland. Widespread throughout Europe. A plant of dry grassland and well-drained soils along roadsides, woodland rides and sand dunes.

Similar species: Lesser Centaury, *C. pulchellum*, is a local species with a more southern distribution. It looks like a smaller version of Common Centaury but has no basal rosette of leaves and clearly stalked flowers. Seaside Centaury, *C. littorale*, is a plant of northern and western coasts. It has strap-like stem leaves.

YELLOW-WORT

Blackstonia perfoliata

Characteristics: An erect, smooth annual, growing up to 45cm. The whole plant is a glaucous grey-green. The leaves are oval-shaped and in a rosette at the base. The paired stem leaves are joined at the base so that the stem looks like it goes through the middle, appearing to form a circle around the stem, hence the species name *perfoliata*, meaning 'through the leaves'. The branching stems at the top have terminal clusters of bright yellow flowers (10-15mm across) with 6 to 8 flat lobes. The calyx is deeply divided, appearing to consist of narrow pointed teeth. The flowers close in the afternoon.

Range and habitat: A widely scattered plant in southern England with a more coastal distribution in the north and west. It is most familiar as a plant of chalk and limestone grassland and scrub, but also calcareous dunes.

Similar species: Easily recognised by its pairs of waxy 'fused' leaves and yellow gentian-like flowers.

AUTUMN GENTIAN

Gentiana amarella

Characteristics: An upright, hairless, tightly-branching perennial, up to 30cm tall. The opposite pairs of leaves are lance-shaped and pointed. The spikes of flowers, which arise from the leaf axils, are in branched clusters. The dull purple flowers have long, upright corolla tubes with 5-pointed lobes at the mouth; up to 10mm across. There is a pale fringe of hairs at the 'throat' of the flower. The calyx has 4 to 5 long teeth of equal length.

Range and habitat: A widespread plant found principally in southern England, although locally common in parts of Wales and Scotland and Ireland. Found widely in northern and central Europe, rarer towards the south. A plant of well-drained basic soils, including short turf on chalk and limestone grassland and calcareous dunes.

Similar species: In the north of Britain on acid grassland, the more likely gentian to be found is the Field Gentian, *G. campestris*, which has bluer flowers and uneven-sized calyx teeth, the larger ones overlapping the smaller. The very local Chiltern Gentian, *G. germanica*, has larger flowers which are more than twice as long as the calyx.

CHANGING FORGET-ME-NOT

Myosotis discolor

Characteristics: A delightful little downy annual up to 20cm tall. The leaves are strap-shaped, forming a basal rosette with a few with pointed tips up the stem. The long, flowering spike is leafless and curling under in bud. The tiny flowers (2mm across) open yellow and gradually turn blue. The outside of the calyx tube is hairy. The corolla tube is twice as long as the calyx.

Range and habitat: A widespread plant throughout the British Isles, less common in Wales and Ireland. Widespread in Europe from Scandinavia southwards. A locally common plant of dry soils on heathland, field edges, roadsides and waste ground.

Similar species: Early Forget-me-not, *M. ramosissima*, is very similar and can grow in similar habitats. It tends to flower earlier in the year and its corolla tube is half as long as the calyx. The fruiting spike is longer than the leafy part of the plant.

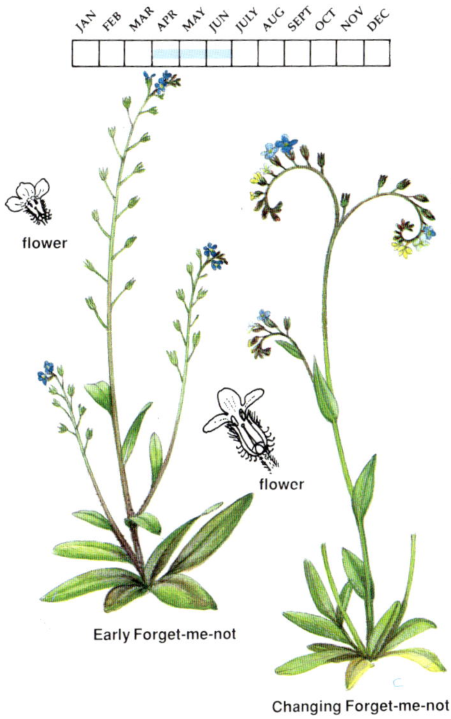

VIPER'S BUGLOSS

Echium vulgare

Characteristics: An erect, coarsely hairy biennial growing up to 90cm with striking blue flowers. The large basal leaves are very hairy and have short stalks. They are lance-shaped to strap-shaped. Those leaves on the stem are stalkless and more pointed. The main stem is covered with bristles. The flowers are in tightly-curled clusters up the main stem, typically with only a few fully open at any one time. The flowers are reddish in bud, opening out into a vivid blue, trumpet-shaped flower with the upper lobes larger than the lower and long, red protruding stamens.

Range and habitat: Widespread in the British Isles as far north as mid-Scotland, tending to have a coastal distribution in the north and west of its range. A plant of dry, bare or disturbed ground on light soils. Often found on shingle and sand dunes, as well as chalk downland in the south.

Similar species: A highly distinctive and unmistakable plant in flower.

GREAT MULLEIN

Verbascum thapsus

Characteristics: A prominent, very 'woolly' biennial, growing up to 2m tall. The large, oval, grey-green leaves form a dense rosette at the base of the plant and a series of alternate leaves enclosing the bottom half of the stem. The terminal flowering spike consists of a dense mass of yellow flowers opening first from the base to give it a conical look. Each flower has 5 flat lobes.

Range and habitat: Widespread in England and Wales but rare in southern Scotland and Ireland. Absent from areas of northern Scotland. Found throughout Europe. A plant of sunny hedgebanks and roadsides and waste ground on light, often disturbed, soils.

Similar species: The other mullein likely to be encountered is the Dark Mullein, *V. nigrum*, which has a more southerly distribution and is confined to similar habitats on calcareous soils. It is not so hairy and has noticeable purple hairs on the orange stamens, making the yellow flowers look as if they have dark centres.

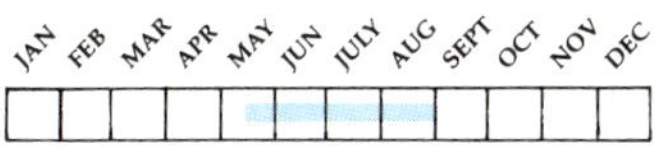

HEATH SPEEDWELL

Veronica officinalis

Characteristics: A creeping perennial with stems hairy all around (see Germander Speedwell, p.35). The leaves are oval with shallow teeth. The flowers are in a long-stalked, erect, pyramidal spike (up to 15cm) arising from the leaf axils. The delicate, pale blue or lilac flowers, (up to 6mm across) with unequal lobes, have short stalks (2mm). The fruit is bigger than the calyx.

Range and habitat: Widespread throughout the British Isles and Europe. A common plant, sometimes forming extensive patches, found on acidic, dry grassland, including heaths, woodland rides and pastures.

Similar species: See p. 35 for descriptions of Germander and Wood Speedwells. Thyme-leaved Speedwell, *V. serpyllifolia*, can be found on acid soils, but is easily separated as it is hairless, its oval leaves are untoothed and its pale blue flowers are in a loose, leafy spike.

YELLOW RATTLE

Rhinanthus minor

Characteristics: An erect, more or less hairless annual which can be very variable, ranging from 10-50cm in height. The stem is spotted with black and is often branched. The toothed leaves are narrow and pointed in stalkless pairs up the stem. The spikes of flowers have leaf-like bracts; the flowers are often in pairs, facing opposite directions. The corolla is a hooded primrose-yellow, with two dark, violet-tipped teeth at the mouth. The calyx is large and flattened vertically, becoming inflated in fruit. When ripe, the seeds 'rattle' inside the calyx – hence the name. It is said that farmers knew the hay was ready to cut when the seeds were 'rattling'. It is a semi-parasite and takes some of its nutrients from the roots of surrounding grasses.

Range and habitat: Widespread throughout the British Isles and Europe. A classic plant of old meadows and pastures, fens and calcareous dunes, usually on neutral to basic soils.

Similar species: The inflated calyx and hooded yellow flower are diagnostic.

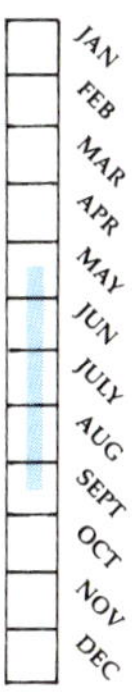

EYEBRIGHT

Euphrasia officinalis agg.

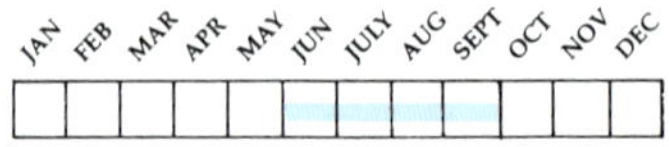

Characteristics: An attractive, variable, low-growing, branched annual growing up to 20cm tall. There are, in fact, many microspecies of this plant. The tiny opposite leaves, sometimes tinged purple, are broadly oval in shape and are coarsely toothed. The miniature, orchid-like flowers (up to 7.5mm long) are in a leafy spike and are white with the lower lobes streaked with purple, with an orangey-yellow blotch at the mouth.

Range and habitat: The most widespread species of this plant is *E. nemersa*, which is found throughout the British Isles and Europe. It is found in a wide range of short grassland communities, from well-drained, acid grassland and chalk downs to woodland rides and coastal dunes. Many of the more local species are confined to upland areas or coastal sites.

Similar species: The low-growing habit and pretty little flowers make this group very distinctive. Separating the many microspecies, however, is a different matter and requires close examination of all parts of the plant. It is worthwhile getting down and having a closer look just to appreciate the beauty of this often overlooked plant.

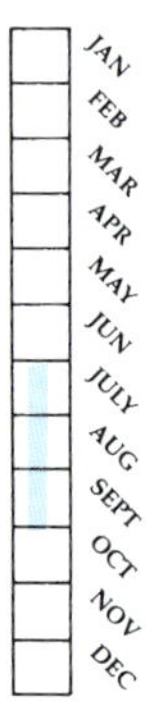

VERVAIN

Verbena officinalis

Characteristics: Our only member of the mostly tropical Verbenaceae family which includes many showy garden shrubs and herbs, as well as trees such as Teak. Our Vervain, however, is a rather insignificant plant: it is a hairy, upright perennial, the stalk is square and up to 60cm tall. The leaves are in opposite pairs and pinnately-lobed and toothed. The long, leafless flower-spikes arise from leaf axils in the top half of the plant and tend to only have a few flowers open at any one time. The pale lilac flowers have a long corolla tube and open lobes, but are only about 4mm across, and easily overlooked.

Range and habitat: A local plant found throughout England and Wales and southern Ireland, though rare north of the Wash. It is a plant of well-drained, calcareous soils found along trackways, hedgebanks and scrub as well as waste ground.

Similar species: None.

MARJORAM

Origanum vulgare

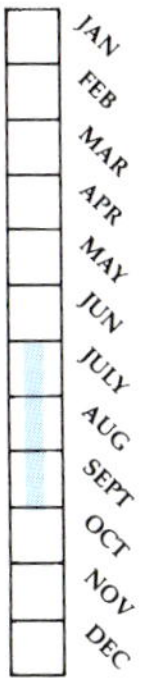

Characteristics: A downy, upright, branching perennial up to 60cm tall. The opposite pairs of shortly-stalked, oval leaves are highly aromatic. The densely clustered flowerheads have purplish, leaf-like bracts. The pinkish flowers contrast with the darker bracts and have a longer upper lip and 3-lobed lower lip with protruding purple stamens. The marjoram grown in gardens are Mediterranean species, *O. onites*, and *O. majorana*. Its strongly-scented flowers are highly attractive to butterflies.

Range and habitat: A widespread species throughout the British Isles, although absent from regions in north Scotland. It is most common in the south. Widespread in central and southern Europe. It is a plant of well-drained, mostly calcareous soils and is found usually along hedgebanks and the scrubby edges of pastures.

Similar species: Told from other aromatic members of the labiate family by the densely packed flowerheads and protruding stamens.

WILD THYME

Thymus praecox

Characteristics: A low, creeping, shrubby plant, sometimes forming a dense mat, up to 7cm tall. The flowering stems are square in cross section, with two opposite sides hairy. The small, oval leaves are opposite and have prominent veins underneath. When crushed they are only slightly aromatic. The purple flowers are clustered in tight whorls at the end of the flowering stem and have two lips, the lower one divided into 3 lobes.

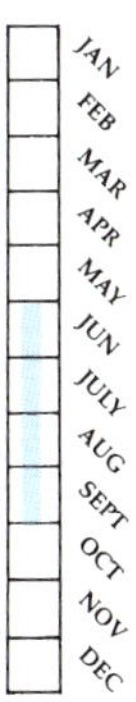

Range and habitat: A widespread plant in the British Isles, though scarce in parts of central England and Ireland. It has a western maritime distribution in Europe. A typical plant of dry, low-cropped grasslands, it is found in a wide range of substrates from cliff tops to sandy heathlands.

Similar species: Large Thyme, *T. pulegioides*, has taller flowering shoots (to 20cm) with a looser flowering-head. The flowering stems have hairs only on the corners. It is more strongly scented than Wild Thyme.

SELFHEAL

Prunella vulgaris

Characteristics: A slightly downy perennial with creeping stems and erect flowering shoots to 20cm. The leaves are untoothed, oval-shaped and pointed; the lower ones are stalked. The flowers are in a dense, oblong, terminal spike with dark, purply-coloured bracts and calyx. The corolla tube is violet with the top lip concave and hooded and the lower lip toothed. The plant is not aromatic. It was widely thought to cure a wide range of wounds and illnesses, hence its common name.

Range and habitat: A very widespread and common plant found right across the Northern Hemisphere. It is found in a wide range of grassland habitats from woodland rides and old meadows to roadsides, garden lawns and waste ground. It usually prefers neutral to basic soils.

Similar species: Sometimes confused with Bugle (see p. 39) but this has blue flowers without a hooded upper lip and blunt-tipped leaves; it also flowers earlier in the year.

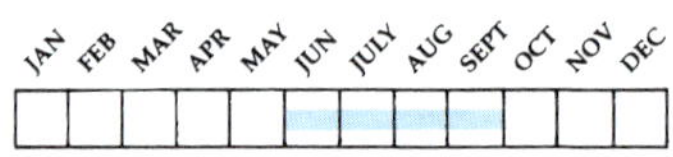

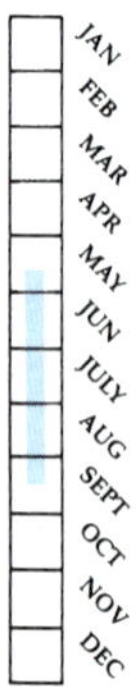

RIBWORT PLANTAIN

Plantago lanceolata

Characteristics: An erect, downy perennial with the flower stalks up to 45cm tall. The rather upright leaves are in a basal rosette and are narrow and spear-shaped, narrowing gradually into a long stalk. The 3 to 5 more or less parallel veins are prominent. The edges of the leaves are only slightly toothed. The cone-shaped flowerhead is held on the end of a long, leafless, square-furrowed stalk. The tiny flowers (4mm across) consist of 4 white sepals and 4 brown petals with long white stamens. It is wind-pollinated.

Range and habitat: Found throughout the British Isles and Europe. A common plant of a range of grasslands from meadows and rough grassland to lawns and roadside verges, usually on slightly acid to basic soils.

Similar species: Told from the other predominantly inland species, Hoary Plantain and Greater Plantain, by the narrow leaves and the furrowed flower stalk. Buckshorn Plantain has lobed leaves and Sea Plantain fleshy leaves which are not so prominently veined.

HOARY PLANTAIN

Plantago media

Characteristics: An erect, downy perennial with the flowerhead up to 40cm tall. The leaves form a flat rosette of oval to round-shaped leaves (up to 10cm long) gradually narrowing into short stalks. The leaves have 5 to 9 veins and are covered in fine whitish hairs, giving them a greyish appearance. The flowerhead is often longer than Ribwort Plantain and consists of many tiny (2mm across) white flowers with pale pink stamens on purple filaments. The flowers are scented as this species, unlike the other plantains, is pollinated by insects.
Range and habitat: A more southern species than Ribwort Plantain, being found widely in England and Europe but less frequent as you move north and west. It is absent from much of Scotland and Ireland but has been introduced in some districts. It is found on basic soils, being most common on calcareous grassland.
Similar species: The pinkish, scented flowerhead distinguish it immediately from other plantains.

HAREBELL

Campanula rotundifolia

Characteristics: An attractive, almost hairless, perennial with upright flower stalks, up to 40cm tall. The creeping stolons produce long-stalked, round to heart-shaped leaves which soon wither. The stem leaves are narrow and strap-shaped, the upper ones are unstalked. The flowers are in drooping, widely-spaced clusters. The individual flowers are pale blue and bell-shaped with 5 oval lobes. The calyx teeth are very fine and spreading. In Scotland this delightful plant is known as the 'bluebell'.
Range and habitat: Widespread in England, Wales and Scotland but rare in the south-west of England. In Ireland it is less common in the south. Widespread in Europe. A plant of dry grasslands on a wide range of soils, being found on both calcareous downs and acid heaths. Also an early colonizer of shallow soils on cliff faces.
Similar species: Told from the other bellflowers (*Campanula*) by the combination of strap-shaped stem leaves and the rounded root leaves.

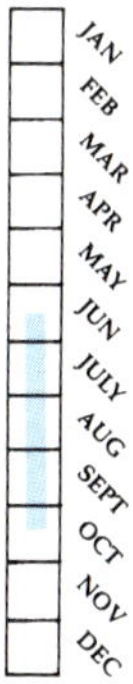

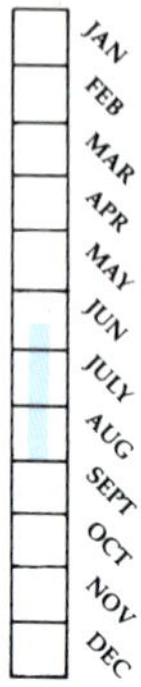

LADY'S BEDSTRAW

Galium verum

Characteristics: A scrambling, branching perennial with more or less erect flowering stems to 60cm tall. The stems are bluntly 4-angled and only slightly hairy. The leaves are in whorls of 8 to 10 up the stem, strap-shaped and pointed, with a single vein. They are a dark green above and paler below, with in-rolled edges. The dense clusters of flowers are in a loose panicle in the upper half of the flowering stem. The tiny (2-4mm across) flowers are a bright yellow with 4 pointed lobes. The rounded fruits are smooth, turning black when ripe. The plant smells of new-mown hay (coumarin), and was once used as a bedding herb.

Range and habitat: Found throughout the British Isles and Europe. A common plant of grassland on a wide range of soils from slightly acid to calcareous soils, often found on rough grassland on old commons and hedge banks and stabilised sand dunes.

Similar species: Told from the other bedstraws by its combination of yellow flowers and narrow leaves.

FIELD SCABIOUS

Knautia arvensis

Characteristics: A hairy, perennial, up to 100cm tall. Basal leaves undivided or with pinnate side lobes; stem leaves deeply pinnate with narrow, pointed sides lobes and a more oval end lobe. The long-stalked flowerheads are pincushion-shaped and 3-4cm wide with around 50 individual lilac-coloured flowers. The outer flowers have larger lobes than the inner ones. The pink anthers protrude beyond the flowers.

Range and habitat: Found throughout the British Isles but rare in northern and western Scotland. A plant of dry, basic soils, often found along open hedgebanks and rough grassland.

Similar species: Small Scabious, *Scabiosa columbaria*, is a smaller, less hairy plant with strap-like lobes on the stem leaves. Also has long, bristle-like calyx teeth. A plant of calcareous grassland. Devil's-bit Scabious, *Succisa pratensis*, has opposite pairs of pointed, oval undivided leaves and dark purplish flowers with equal-sized lobes. It is a plant of damp meadows and woodland rides, fens, and drier basic soils.

COMMON RAGWORT

Senecio jacobaea

Characteristics: An upright, branching, yellow-flowered member of the daisy family, up to 150cm tall. It is a biennial. The basal leaves form a rosette and are pinnately-lobed; the lobes have widely-spaced, pointed teeth, the end lobe usually being larger and blunt. The stem leaves have narrower lobes, the uppermost clasping the stem. They are sometimes cottony below and dark green above. The flowerheads are in dense, branching terminal clusters. Each yellow flowerhead is up to 25mm across with an inner disc of tightly-packed florets and an outer circle of strap-shaped ray florets.

Range and habitat: Found throughout the British Isles and Europe. A very common and troublesome weed of overgrazed and neglected pasture, roadsides, waste ground and sand dunes.

Similar species: There are several similar species of ragwort. The most similar is the Hoary Ragwort, *S. erucifolius*, but this has distinctly felted or cottony undersides to the leaves and the whole plant is a grey-green colour. The end lobe is usually narrow and pointed and the flowers are a uniform pale yellow. See also Oxford Ragwort (p.152).

COMMON FLEABANE

Pulicaria dysenterica

Characteristics: An upright, hairy, perennial member of the daisy family, growing up to 60cm. The leaves are lance-shaped with those up the stem having heart-shaped bases that clasp the stem. The golden yellow flowerheads are held in a loose, branching, flat-topped cluster with each flowerhead 1.5-3cm across, with the ray florets twice as long as the disc florets. The name 'Fleabane' comes from its use for centuries, when dried and burned, as a deterrent against fleas. It was also meant to act as a cure for dysentry, hence the species name.

Range and habitat: Found throughout England, Wales and southern Scotland; a widespread plant in Ireland. Widespread in Europe. A common plant of damp grassland, ditches and marshes, particularly on clay, where its summer-flowering heads can appear to dominate the scene.

Similar species: The woolly, clasping leaves distinguish it from most other yellow daisy flowers.

DAISY

Bellis perennis

Characteristics: One of our most familiar wild flowers, used as a decorative plant by children and worried over as a persistent weed of lawns by adults. It is a low-growing perennial up to 18cm tall, but usually around 5cm. The downy leaves are spoon-shaped and slightly toothed, in a basal rosette. The solitary flowerheads are carried on leafless stalks. The flower is 16-25mm across with white ray florets, sometimes tinged pink, and many disc florets. The seed does not have a pappus of hairs like many other members of this family, however; it usually spreads vegetatively.

Range and habitat: Widespread throughout the British Isles and Europe. An abundant plant of short grassland, on a wide range of soil types, only avoiding very acid conditions. Can thrive in heavily grazed and trampled grassland giving it a competitive edge over other plants.

Similar species: The only low-growing yellow and white flowered 'daisy' with spoon-shaped leaves.

YARROW

Achillea millefolium

Characteristics: A hairy, upright (to 40cm) perennial with creeping runners; it is highly aromatic. The fern-like leaves are 2 to 3 times pinnate with narrow leaflets, and are usually lance-shaped, the upper leaves shorter. The flowerheads are small but numerous, forming a flat-topped 'umbel'-like cluster. The cream-coloured flowerhead is 4-6mm in diameter with 5 broad ray florets and a dense centre of disc florets. The flowerheads are sometimes a pinkish colour.

Range and habitat: Widespread and common in the British Isles and Europe. A sometimes abundant plant of grasslands on a wide range of soils, but most noticeable in extensive patches on unkempt lawns and roadsides.

Similar species: The combination of dense, flat-topped 'umbels' of flowers and feathery leaves readily distinguish this plant. A near relative, Sneezewort, *A. ptarmica*, has larger flowerheads borne in a looser cluster and narrow, lance-shaped, finely-toothed leaves. It is a plant of damp, acid grasslands.

OX-EYE DAISY

Leucanthemum vulgare

Characteristics: An erect perennial, looking rather like a large daisy, growing up to 70cm. It has a basal rosette of dark green, spoon-shaped leaves with toothed edges, and along the stem it has widely-spaced, oblong leaves which are pinnately lobed and clasp the stem. The flowerheads are borne singly on long stalks and are up to 5cm in diameter. The ray florets are long and white and the disc florets are yellow. This familiar roadside plant has a host of common names, of which Geoffrey Grigson lists over 60 in *The Englishman's Flora*, including Moon Daisy, Thunder Daisy and Dog Daisy.

Range and habitat: Widely distributed throughout the British Isles and Europe, less common in Scotland. A common and sometimes abundant plant of grassy places from roadside verges and hedgebanks to meadows and cliff tops. It is most prolific on fertile soils.

Similar species: The Mayweeds have similar but smaller flowerheads and have deeply dissected, feathery leaves with narrow, strap-shaped segments.

MUSK THISTLE

Carduus nutans

Characteristics: An erect, cottony biennial, growing up to 100cm. The stem has spiny edges but is spineless below the flowerhead. The leaves all have very spiny edges; the lower leaves are broadly oval-shaped with wavy margins, the upper leaves are narrower and deeply lobed. They are hairy above and woolly below. The flowerheads are usually carried singly and droop gracefully to one side. They are fragrant and form large, round, reddish-purple discs of florets up to 5cm across. The bracts are long, spiny and purplish in colour; the outer bracts are curved backwards.

Range and habitat: Most common in England becoming rarer in the north and west but found as far north as the Moray Firth and in Ireland along the coast in Galway. In Europe, it is commoner in the south but is found as far north as southern Scandinavia. It is a plant of well-drained calcareous soils, frequently found along field edges, roadsides and waste ground, as well as pastures.

Similar species: The large, drooping flowerheads with the large, recurved bracts distinguish the Musk Thistle from other thistles.

CREEPING THISTLE

Cirsium arvense

Characteristics: A familiar, hairless perennial growing up to 90cm, with creeping side roots from which arise numerous shoots. The flowering stems are unwinged and spineless. The leaves are lance-shaped in outline, with very wavy lobed edges with many spines. The upper sides of the leaves are hairless; sometimes cottony underneath. The flowerheads are in a loose cluster of 2 to 4. The flowerhead itself is globular to egg-shaped with pale lilac florets. The bracts are tinged purple and are held flat against the side of the flowerhead. The plant is usually dioecious.

Range and habitat: An ubiquitous weed found throughout the British Isles and Europe. A troublesome weed of pasture and arable land, gardens, roadsides and waste ground.

Similar species: The only thistle with globular lilac flowerheads and spineless stems. The Spear Thistle (see p. 156) has much bigger purple flowers and has overwintering rosettes of basal leaves.

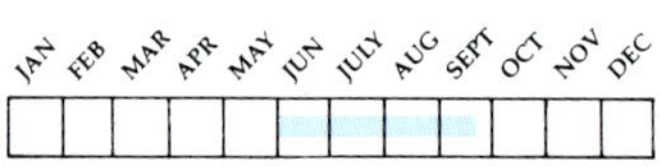

STEMLESS THISTLE

Cirsium acaulon

Characteristics: A low-growing perennial, seldom over 6cm tall, when not in flower is often overlooked but is soon discovered when sat upon! The plant consists of a prostrate rosette of lance-shaped leaves which are pinnately-lobed and have stiff, wavy edges covered in spines. The flowerheads are usually sessile and number 1 to 3, arising from the centre of the rosette. The florets are reddish-purple and deeply lobed. The bracts are all pressed against the base of the flowerhead. The flower is pollinated by bees and other insects.

Range and habitat: Widespread in central, southern and eastern England as far as Yorkshire and south Wales. Found through central and western Europe as far north as southern Scandinavia. A classic plant of short, grazed, calcareous pasture, particularly on well-drained, south-facing slopes.

Similar species: The only British thistle with stemless flowerheads.

GREATER KNAPWEED

Centaurea scabiosa

Characteristics: An upright, branching, slightly downy perennial growing up to 90cm. The basal leaves are large (up to 25cm long) and have deep pinnate lobes. The stem leaves are stalkless but also lobed. The flowerhead is large (up to 5cm across) with bright reddish-purple florets. Those on the outside of the flowerhead are longer and spread outwards. The bracts around the globular base of the flowerhead have a darker fringed horseshoe-shaped top to them, giving the head a distinct patterned look. The fruit has a pappus of stiff white hairs.

Range and habitat: Widely scattered throughout most of the British Isles except north-west Scotland. In the west and north it is primarily a coastal plant. Widespread in Europe. A plant of dry grasslands and hedgebanks.

Similar species: Common Knapweed, *C. nigra,* is similar but is smaller, usually lacks the spreading outer florets, the leaves are lance-shaped and not deeply lobed, the bracts have darker, triangular-shaped appendages.

CAT'S-EAR

Hypochoeris radicata

Characteristics: The yellow dandelion-like flowers contain some very confusing groups of plants. Only a few easily recognised species are described here. Cat's-ear is an erect perennial growing up to 60cm tall. It has a rosette of basal leaves which are lance-shaped in outline and bluntly toothed. The leaves are covered in bristly hairs. The flowering stems are either simple or sparingly branched. They have small, brown-tipped, scale-like bracts up the stem. The flowerhead is bright yellow, with the outer florets greenish-grey beneath. The fruit has a pappus of hairs which have feathery side branches.

Range and habitat: Found throughout the British Isles and Europe. A common plant of a wide range of grasslands on neutral to mildly acid soils.

Similar species: Smooth Cat's-ear, *H. glabra,* as its name suggests, has smooth leaves and a smaller flowerhead. A scattered species of sandy soils. See also Autumn Hawkbit (overleaf).

AUTUMN HAWKBIT

Leontodon autumnalis

Characteristics: A dandelion-like perennial usually up to 40cm tall. The leaves are in a basal rosette and are deeply pinnately-lobed, rather like dandelion leaves; they are either hairless or have a few hairs. The flowering stems are branched 2 or 3 times and taper into the flowerhead, which has golden-yellow florets, the outer ones of which are reddish beneath. The fruit has a pappus of white, branching hairs.

Range and habitat: A common plant found throughout the British Isles and Europe. A plant of a wide range of grasslands from roadsides and commons, to meadows and mountain scree. It is most characteristic of calcareous grassland.

Similar species: Told from Cat's-ear by the tapering flowerhead and the absence of dark-tipped bracts along the stem. The Rough Hawkbit, *L. hispidus*, is very hairy; the leaves and stem are covered with Y-shaped hairs; the stem is unbranched. Also the flowerhead narrows abruptly into the stem.

GOAT'S-BEARD

Tragopogon pratensis

Characteristics: A tall, hairless dandelion-like annual or perennial, up to 70cm tall. The basal leaves are grey-green, long and pointed, almost grass-like, and are wider at the base forming a loose sheath around the stem. The stem leaves are more upright. The flowering stem is long and hairless, sometimes branched, with a single flowerhead at the top. The pale yellow flower only opens during the morning, hence the other common name, Jack-go-to-bed-at-noon. The long, pointed bracts are usually longer than the outer florets, giving it a 'spiky' appearance. The pappus is very large resembling a large, downy 'dandelion-clock'.

Range and habitat: Widespread throughout the British Isles; rare in the west and absent in parts of northern of Scotland. A plant of roadside verges, hedgebanks and rough grassland.

Similar species: The grass-like, grey-green leaves distinguish Goat's-beard from other dandelion-like species. The introduced Salsify, *T. porrifolius*, is similar but has blue florets.

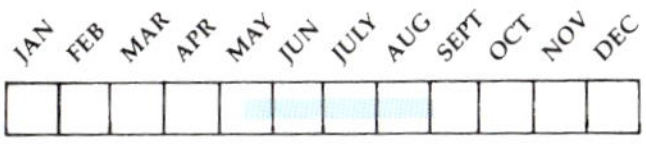

MOUSE-EARED HAWKWEED

Hieracium pilosella

Characteristics: The hawkweeds are one of the most complex groups of plants to identify accurately with as many as perhaps 250 microspecies in Britain alone. Mouse-eared Hawkweed, however, is a common plant that is relatively easy to identify. It has leafy basal runners and a basal rosette of oval-shaped, untoothed leaves covered in white hairs, felted beneath. The flowering stem (up to 30cm) is also hairy and unbranched, with a solitary lemon-yellow flowerhead. The outer florets are tinged reddish beneath.

Range and habitat: A widespread plant in the British Isles and Europe, absent from areas of northern Scotland. A common plant of short grassland on a wide range of soils including pasture, roadsides, hedgebanks, sand dunes and waste ground.

Similar species: Rough Hawkbit is a much larger plant with Y-shaped hairs. For those who want the challenge of identifying the various groups, a good start is the *Excursion Flora* published by Cambridge University Press.

SMOOTH HAWK'S-BEARD

Crepis capillaris

Characteristics: A usually hairless, erect, branching annual, up to 90cm tall. The basal leaves form a rosette of dandelion-like, pointed, pinnately-lobed leaves. The stem leaves are smaller and arrow-shaped, clasping the stem. The small flowerheads (up to 5mm across) are in loosely branched clusters. The bracts form a cup-shaped base and the florets are bright yellow, reddish beneath. The fruits have a simple pappus of white hairs.

Range and habitat: Found throughout the British Isles and in Europe north to southern Scandinavia. A very common plant of dry grasslands including pastures, heaths, roadsides.

Similar species: Rough Hawk's-beard, *C. biennis*, is a more local plant of the south and east of Britain. It is larger (up to 120cm) and more hairy, without the arrow-shaped lobes to the stem leaves. Marsh Hawk's-beard, *C. paludosa*, has toothed but not deeply-lobed leaves and golden-yellow florets. The pappus is brown. Found in northern wet meadows and marshes.

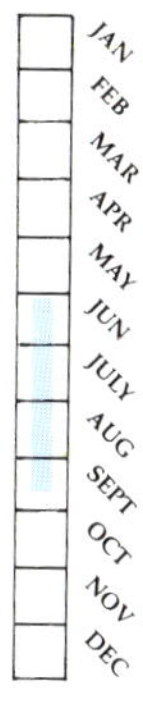

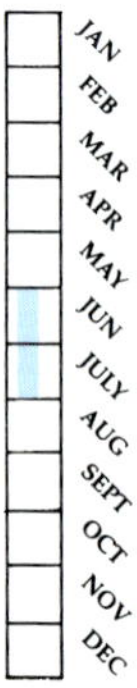

FRAGRANT ORCHID

Gymnodenia conopsea

Characteristics: An upright, hairless orchid, growing up to 40cm tall. The leaves are long (up to 15cm), narrow and unspotted and glossy green in colour. They are keeled and hooded at the tip, growing in two ranks up the stem. The upper stem leaves are bract-like. The flowering spike is long (up to 10cm) and densely flowered. The reddish-pink flowers (up to 12mm wide) have spreading outer sepals and a lower lip with three equal lobes. The upper sepal and two petals form a small hood. A long (up to 20mm) curved spur protrudes from the back of the flower. A larger and more robust subspecies, *densiflora*, has clove-scented flowers and grows in fens and damper habitats.

Range and habitat: Widespread throughout the British Isles and Europe. A plant mainly of dry calcareous grassland in the south. In the north it can be found in damp pastures.

Similar species: The Pyramidal Orchid has a pyramidal flowering spike and a distinctly 3-lobed lower lip.

BEE ORCHID

Ophrys apifera

Characteristics: A rather exotic-looking orchid, growing up to 50cm. The oval to oblong basal leaves are grey-green and pointed, forming a rosette. A few smaller leaves grow up the stem. The loose-flowering spike has 2 to 7 flowers. The flower itself consists of 3, large, pointed sepals, usually a pale pink colour; the upper petals are small, greenish-brown and square-ended. The large, hairy lower lip resembles the back of a female bumble-bee, having a pattern (often U-shaped) of yellow or cream over a chestnut brown background.

Range and habitat: Found widely throughout England, Wales and Ireland, becoming increasingly rare to the west and north. Widespread in central and southern Europe. A local plant principally of short calcareous turf but also found in quarries and dunes.

Similar species: The Fly Orchid, *O. insectifera*, has a long, slender flower spike with antennae-like upper petals and a brown and purple coloured lower lip supposedly resembling a fly.

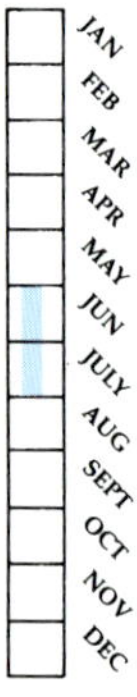

flower

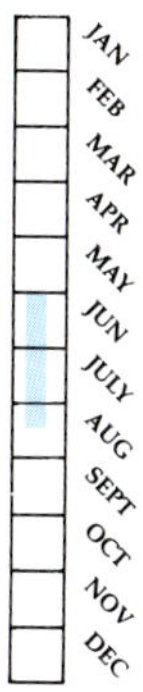

COMMON SPOTTED ORCHID

Dactylorhiza fuchsii

Characteristics: This is the orchid that is most likely to be encountered. An erect plant growing up to 50cm tall with a rosette of oval to oblong spotted leaves. The stem leaves are small and pointed. The dense flower spike is pyramidal at first, later becoming cylindrical. The attractive pink flowers have spreading outer sepals and the upper petals form a 'cowl'. The lower lip is marked with a looping pattern of purple streaks and dots and has 3 equal lobes, the centre one of which is dagger-shaped.

Range and habitat: Widespread throughout the British Isles and Europe. Most common in the south and east where it can be an abundant plant on a wide range of habitats from dune slacks and fens to scrub and woodland rides, even roadside verges, on base-rich soils.

Similar species: Heath Spotted Orchid is very similar (see p. 119). The Marsh Orchids, *D. praetermissa* and *D. purpurella,* have unspotted leaves and a larger, less divided lower lip.

PYRAMIDAL ORCHID

Anacamptis pyramidalis

Characteristics: An erect, hairless orchid, growing up to 45cm tall. The leaves are unspotted, lance-shaped and pointed, arranged spirally up the stem. Those higher up are much smaller and bract-like. The dense flower spike is pyramidal initially, opening out into more of a dome-shaped cluster. The flowers are wholly pink with the upper petals and sepals forming a curving hood. The lip has three equal-sized deep lobes and a long, pink spur, as long as the ovary, protrudes from the rear. The flower has a fox-like smell.

Range and habitat: Widespread throughout the British Isles, through most common in the south, and in Europe north to southern Scandinavia. A locally common and sometimes abundant plant of base-rich soils from chalk and limestone grassland to dune slacks and cliff tops.

Similar species: Sometimes confused with Fragrant Orchid but this has a much taller, cylindrical flowering spike and paler, more lilac-coloured flowers.

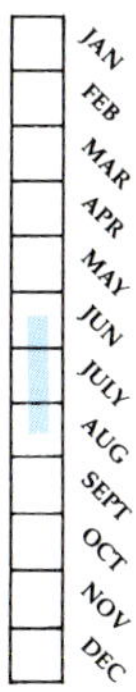

flower

RIVERS, LAKES AND MARSHES

Our wetland areas contain some of our most fragile and threatened habitats. Subjected to centuries of drainage and manipulation by man, in recent decades they have also suffered from pollution and increasing recreational pressures. The plant life of these habitats is highly varied and contains some of our most beautiful and exotic flowers, such as the water-lilies and Yellow Flag, as well as highly specialised plants such as the bladderworts.

Rivers can support an interesting succession of plants, depending on the quality of the water and the nature of the flow. For example, fast-flowing, shallow rivers and streams sometimes have rafts of water-crowfoots, with their white, buttercup-like flowers held above the surface, with starworts and Fool's Watercress in the slower-flowing sections. Deeper clay rivers might have Yellow Water-lilies and the bizzare-shaped leaves of Arrowhead along their edges. The fringing plants are equally attractive, with spikes of Purple and Yellow Loosestrife in high summer. Plants from other continents have spread along many of our waterways and include the attractive Monkey Flower and Orange Balsam, as well as the aggressive Indian Balsam and Canadian Pondweed.

Lakes and ponds often share many of the plants that are found in slow-flowing rivers, but the gradual colonisation of the edges by marsh species enables many plants to establish a foothold. The Bogbean is a classic plant of pool edges and marshes, especially in upland areas. Many ponds and natural lakes have been lost over the centuries either through natural encroachment or drainage, but many new ponds and lakes are being created as a result of gravel extraction and, given the right landscaping, can be quickly colonized by waterplants. Our bogs and fens, however, cannot be so easily recreated and are fragile habitats requiring precise conditions to maintain them. As a result, there are few extensive sites in lowland Europe outside nature reserves and other protected areas.

A carpet of Water Crowfoot across a river in northern England.

MARSH MARIGOLD

Caltha palustris

Characteristics: A semi-erect, hairless, robust-looking perennial, growing up to 45cm. The basal leaves are on long stalks and are glossy green and kidney- to heart-shaped. The upper leaves clasp the thick, hollow, flowering stems. The flowers are large (up to 5cm across) and consist of 5, bright golden-yellow, petal-like sepals with as many as 100 yellow stamens. The seeds are housed in large pod-like capsules. It has one of the most primitive flowers in Britain.

Range and habitat: Widespread in the British Isles and Europe, reaching 1,100 metres in the Scottish Highlands. It is a classic early-flowering plant of marshy meadows, ditches and wet woodlands, where it can sometimes form spectacular displays along the woodland edges in spring.

Similar species: Difficult to confuse with any other species. Greater Spearwort, *Ranunculus lingua,* is a marsh plant with large, glossy, yellow flowers but is much taller with long, narrow leaves and flowers with green sepals.

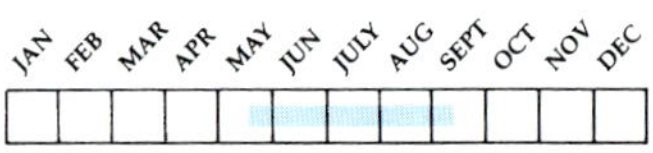

CELERY-LEAVED BUTTERCUP

Ranunculus sceleratus

Characteristics: A hairless, erect, branching annual, growing up to 60cm tall. The long-stalked, lower leaves are a shiny green, 3-lobed and bluntly toothed. The stem-leaves are narrower, lobed and without teeth. The pale yellow flowers are carried in branching clusters and are small (5-10mm across). The sepals are recurved. The fruits form distinctive cylindrical heads, like miniature, green pineapples.

Range and habitat: Widespread in the British Isles but becoming increasingly rare towards the north and west. In Scotland and Ireland it is rare, with a largely coastal distribution. Widespread in Europe. A plant of muddy streams, ditches and pond edges on mineral-rich soils.

Similar species: None of the other buttercups have their fruits in the same shaped head; also the upright, almost bushy, habit and preference for muddy habitats means that it can be quickly distinguished.

LESSER SPEARWORT

Ranunculus flammula

Characteristics: A hairless, creeping to erect perennial, growing up to 50cm tall. Unlike most buttercups the leaves are lance-shaped with those at the base on stalks. The stems are only sparingly branched, occasionally rooting at intervals. The flowers are a glossy yellow with 5 petals and greenish-yellow sepals which clasp the underside of the flower. They are often solitary or in a loose cluster. The fruits form a globular cluster.

Range and habitat: Widespread throughout the British Isles and Europe. Lesser Spearwort is a common plant of marshy places, such as pond edges, ditches, fens and damp woodlands.

Similar species: Great Spearwort is much larger (up to 120cm tall), with long lance-shaped leaves, often over 20cm in length. The flowers are also twice as large. It is a plant of similar habitats but is more restricted to calcium-rich soils and is much more local.

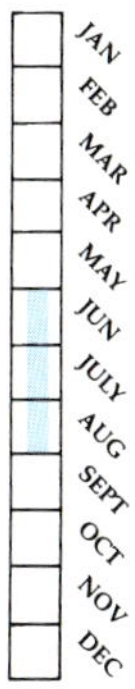

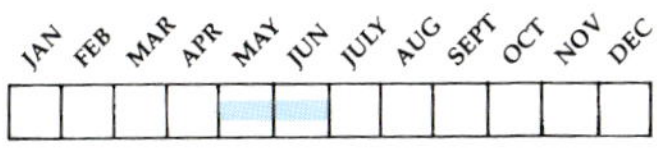

COMMON WATER-CROWFOOT

Ranunculus aquatilis

Characteristics: The water-crowfoot group are a rather confusing aquatic branch of the buttercup family, with white buttercup-like flowers. They are found in a wide variety of aquatic habitats. Common Water-crowfoot, like many others of the group, has two types of leaf: a floating, broadly circular leaf with typically 5 lobes and toothed edges, and submerged bunches of feathery leaves (in some of the fast-flowing river species these can form long plumes of leaves). The flowers are white, tinged yellow towards the centre with many yellow stamens. The head of fruits is globular.

Range and habitat: Widespread throughout most of the British Isles but becoming rarer in the north. A plant most typically of fertile ponds, ditches and streams.

Similar species: Pond Water-crowfoot, *R. peltatus*, is similar but has larger flowers (petals 12-15mm as opposed to 5-10mm) and blunter-toothed leaves. It is also found on less fertile substrates.

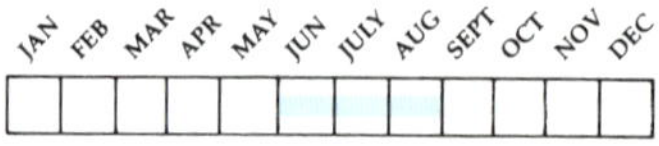

fruit

YELLOW WATER-LILY

Nuphar lutea

Characteristics: A well-known aquatic perennial, with a large, creeping root system. The floating leathery leaves are oval-shaped in outline and are carried on long stalks from the root-base at the bottom of the river or pond. The submerged leaves are on shorter stalks and are thinner and cabbage-like. The large yellow flowers are carried clear of the water and consist of 5 to 6 greenish-yellow sepals and numerous smaller yellow petals inside; the central ovary has a distinctive, flat, disc-like top. The mature flower can smell of alcohol. The seed capsule is shaped like an old-fashion flask, which together with the scent has given the plant the name of Brandy Bottle.

Range and habitat: Widespread throughout the British Isles but absent from parts of northern Scotland and rare in the far south west. Found throughout Europe.

Similar species: In flower the plant is unmistakable. The rare Least Water-lily of northern regions is smaller. The leaves of White Water-lily are rounder.

WHITE WATER-LILY

Nymphaea alba

Characteristics: An attractive aquatic perennial with a large rooting stock. The large, floating leaves are carried on long stalks and are almost circular. There are no submerged leaves. The flowers are very large and showy, up to 20cm across, making them the largest in Britain. They have 4 outer sepals, green on the outside and white on the inside, and 20 to 25 white, oval, pointed petals. Smaller strap-shaped stamens can be seen towards the centre with the bright yellow stigmas. The flower only opens fully in full sunshine and partially submerges at night. The globular, scarred fruit ripens underwater.

Range and habitat: Widespread throughout the British Isles and Europe. A plant of slow-flowing nutrient-rich rivers, lakes and ponds. It can grow in depths of up to 3m. It is not very tolerant of pollution and is more local than the Yellow Water-lily in many lowland regions.

Similar species: The combination of very large circular leaves and white flowers make it unmistakable.

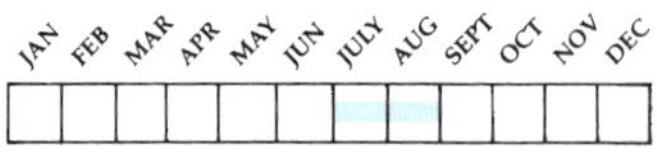

WATERCRESS

Nasturtium officinale

Characteristics: A well-known hairless, aquatic perennial, with stout, hollow stems, widely grown as a salad crop; the semi-erect flowering shoots grow up to 60cm. The pinnate leaves have 5 to 9 pairs of oval leaflets with a larger rounded terminal leaflet. They are not toothed. The flowers are small (4-6mm across) with 4 white petals. The seed pods are cylindrical with two rows of seeds.
Range and habitat: Widespread and common throughout the British Isles, though rarer in the north of Scotland. In Europe it is found north to southern Scandinavia. A sometimes abundant plant of clear, clean water in fertile districts, particularly spring-fed stream heads with a constant supply of water. It has been cultivated since the early 19th Century. Caution should be used in picking wild Watercress as streams and rivers flowing through land with livestock could contain the liver fluke, a parasitic flatworm, which can infect people as well as farm animals.
Similar species: The One-row Watercress, *N. microphylla*, has a single row of seeds in its pods and its leaves turn purplish in autumn, whereas Watercress remains a fresh green. Note that the two species can hybridize. Fool's Watercress is an aquatic member of the carrot family with pinnate leaves but has spear-shaped, toothed leaflets.

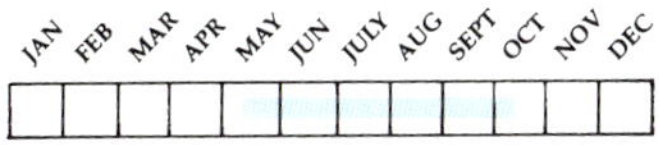

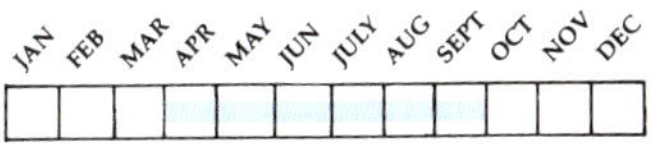

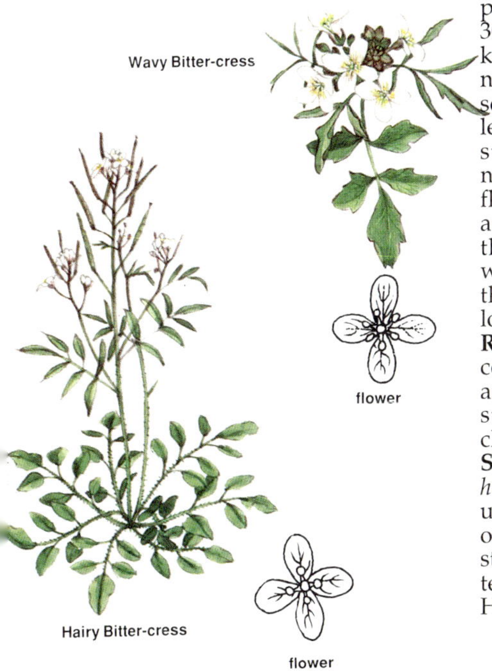

WAVY BITTER-CRESS

Cardamine flexuosa

Characteristics: A common biennial to perennial of stream sides, growing to 30cm tall. It has an erect leafy stem that kinks at each leaf joint, hence the name. The basal leaves form a loose rosette and have about 5 pairs of oval leaflets with a larger end leaflet. The stem leaflets tend to be smaller and narrower. The flowers initially form a flat-topped dense cluster which elongates as the fruits ripen. The flowers themselves consist of 4 white petals, which are twice as long as the sepals; there are 6 stamens. The seed pods are long and point upwards.
Range and habitat: Widespread and common throughout the British Isles and Europe. A typical plant of shady stream sides and damp patches, including roadsides and gardens.
Similar species: Hairy Bittercress, *C. hirsuta*, can look very similar but is usually smaller with a denser rosette of basal leaves, straighter stem and 4 stamens. The main stem of Wavy Bittercress often has 4 to 7 leaves whilst Hairy Bittercress has 1 to 4.

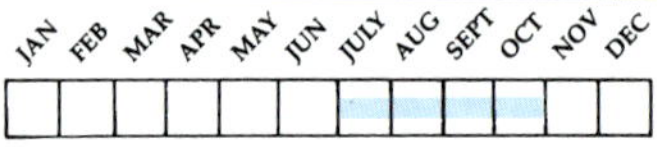

INDIAN BALSAM

Impatiens glandulifera

Characteristics: A large, robust-looking, hairless annual, with stout reddish stems growing up to 2m. An alien introduced from the Himalayas. The leaves are lance-shaped, growing in whorls of 2 or 3, with sharp reddish teeth and long stalks. The flowers arise from the upper leaf-axils and form branching clusters. The pink flowers are large (2.5-4cm long) with a large lower lip, smaller curled back upper lip and a broad spur. The ripe pear-shaped seed pods explode, scattering the seeds, when touched.

Range and habitat: First introduced to Britain in the first half of the 19th Century, it has spread rapidly, particularly in the north and west where in some regions it is the dominant riverside plant. Found on river and stream sides but will also colonise waste ground.

Similar species: The Orange Balsam, *I. capensis*, is smaller and slenderer, with orange flowers. The native, Touch-me-not, *I. noli-tangere*, has a yellow flower and is found locally in the north and west.

GREAT BURNET

Sanguisorba officinalis

Characteristics: A slender, branching, hairless perennial, growing up to 1m tall. Leaves are pinnate with 3 to 7 opposite pairs of stalked, spear-shaped, toothed leaflets, increasing in size towards the tip. Few leaves on the upper flowering stems. The flowers are tiny in a densely packed oblong head 1-2cm long. Each flower has 4, dull, red sepals and 4 stamens as well as a style, unlike Salad Burnet which has mainly separate male and female flowers.

Range and habitat: Found in central and northern England. Rare and local in the south east, in southern Scotland and locally common in parts of Ireland. In Europe it is widespread but scarce. A plant of wet meadows and pastures, fens and marshes. Recent improvement and drainage of these habitats has meant that many populations have been reduced or lost.

Similar species: A much larger and more elegant plant than Salad Burnet.

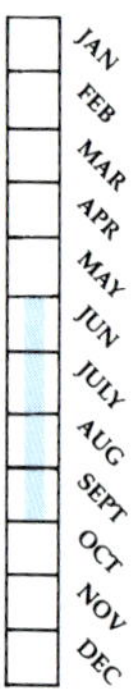

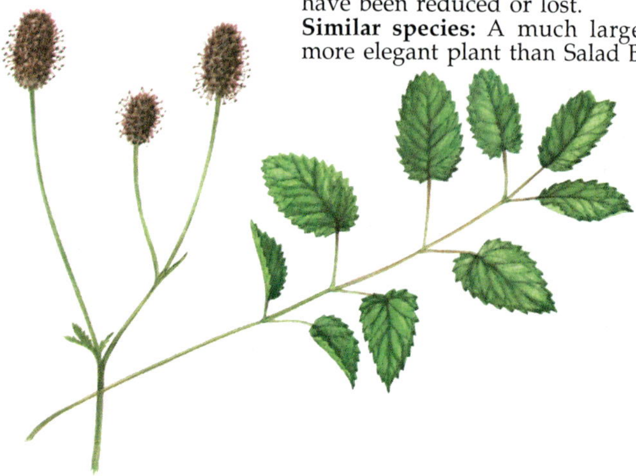

MEADOWSWEET

Filipendula ulmaria

Characteristics: This strongly scented, erect perennial, grows up to 120cm tall. The lower leaves, up to 60cm long, are stalked and consist of 2 to 5 opposite pairs of main leaflets, oval in shape and pointed, with much smaller leaflets in between. There is a large, 3-lobed terminal leaflet. All have two rows of teeth along the edge and are dark, glossy green above and lighter below. The dense head of creamy flowers has many tiny flowers. Each flower is up to 10mm across and has 5 reflexed sepals and petals with many stamens. The fruits are twisted spirally like little, green, butter whorls.

Range and habitat: A widespread plant throughout the British Isles and Europe. A common plant of marshes, streamsides, and damp meadows.

Similar species: See Dropwort (p. 64).

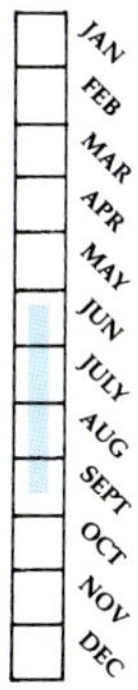

WATER AVENS

Geum rivale

Characteristics: A downy, tufted perennial, growing up to 60cm tall. The basal leaves are pinnate with irregularly-shaped pairs of leaflets; the terminal lobe is usually much larger and rounded. All the leaflets are toothed. The flowers are held in a loose drooping spike. The petals are a dull orange and are held erect giving the appearance of a half-open flower; the sepals are also upright, clasping the petals and are a purple-brown colour. The fruits have long, feathery, hooked tips, forming a dense, globular cluster.

Range and habitat: Widely distributed in the British Isles, though more common in the north and west; it is a scarce plant in southern England. It has a scattered distribution throughout most of Europe. A plant of wet habitats on neutral to basic soils and can be found in marshes and fens, damp woodland rides and wet meadows.

Similar species: The lower leaves could be confused with Herb Bennet (see p. 26). Where the two plants occur together they can produce hybrids.

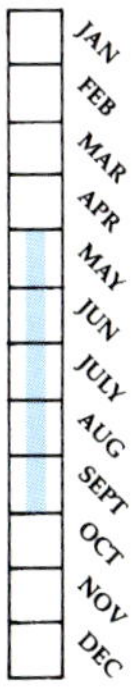

OPPOSITE-LEAVED GOLDEN-SAXIFRAGE

Chrysosplenium oppositifolium

Characteristics: A creeping perennial, forming patches by means of its rooting stems; the erect, leafy flowering shoots grow up to 15cm tall. The rounded leaves are in opposite pairs, tapering or wedge-shaped at the base. The leaf stem is about as long as the leaf blade. The flowers, carried in branching clusters, are tiny, with 4 golden-green sepals surrounded by large, pale yellowish-green bracts.

Range and habitat: Widespread throughout the British Isles; scarce in parts of the east and south of England. Found in west and central Europe as far south as northern Italy. A plant of shady streamsides and flushes, typically on neutral to acid substrates.

Similar species: Alternate-leaved Golden-saxifrage, *C. alternifolium*, is a larger plant with alternate, kidney-shaped rather than opposite leaves on longer stalks. It is a rarer plant, found in similar habitats and sometimes with Opposite-leaved Golden-saxifrage, but more typical on basic rocks.

GRASS-OF-PARNASSUS

Parnassia palustris

Characteristics: An attractive white-flowered plant looking nothing like a grass! It is a hairless, perennial growing up to 30cm tall. The basal leaves are long-stalked and spear-shaped with a single stalkless leaf at the base of the flowering stem. The flowers (up to 30mm across) are carried singly on the long stem and have 5 oval, green-veined, white petals. The flower has 5 fertile stamens and 5 sterile delicately-branched stamens, tipped with yellow glands. The name is supposed to come from the fact that the flower was found by the Greek physician Diosocrides growing on the slopes of Mount Parnassus in Greece.

Range and habitat: A widespread and local plant of northern Britain and Ireland. Found over much of Europe. A declining plant of fens, wet meadows, marshes and wet moorland particularly on basic soils.

Similar species: At first glance it could be mistaken for a white-flowered Saxifrage but the flower and leaves are quite distinct.

GREAT WILLOWHERB

Epilobium hirsutum

Characteristics: A tall, densely hairy perennial, growing up to 150cm tall. The stems are round and covered in spreading hairs. The opposite pairs of leaves are long (to 12cm) and lance-shaped with finely toothed edges; the upper leaves clasp the stem. The flowers are in a loose leafy cluster at the top of the plant. The flowers arise singly from the leaf-axils and have 4 deep purple-pink notched petals with a prominent cream-coloured, 4-lobed stigma; this combination of colours gives the plant its other name of Codlins-and-cream. The fruit is a long pod-like capsule which splits to release many feathery seeds.

Range and habitat: Found throughout the British Isles except for north-west Scotland. Widespread in Europe north to southern Sweden. A common plant of marshes, streamsides and fens, particularly on base-rich soils.

Similar species: Hoary Willowherb, *E. parviflorum*, grows in similar places but is shorter, has a smaller paler flower, and is only hairy towards the stem top.

PURPLE-LOOSESTRIFE

Lythrum salicaria

Characteristics: A distinctive, tall waterside perennial, growing up to 120cm. The stems are erect, usually unbranched and 4-angled, slightly downy. The leaves are in opposite pairs or whorls of three and are stalkless and lance-shaped. The rose-purple flowers are in whorls arising from leaf-like bracts, up a long flowering spike. Each flower has 6 petals with 12 stamens. There are three forms of flower, found on different plants, with the relative lengths of the stamens and style slightly different in each form. This ensures that the insect pollinators can only successfully pollinate flowers from different plants, which helps to maintain the vigour of the species.

Range and habitat: Found throughout the British Isles except for northern Scotland where it is restricted to the west coast. A typical river bankside plant; also found in the marginal vegetation of ponds, marshes and fens.

Similar species: Similar to Rosebay Willowherb from a distance but the 6-petalled flowers are distinctive.

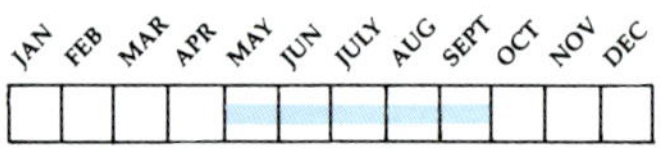

COMMON STARWORT

Callitriche stagnalis

Characteristics: A variable water plant, which can be annual or perennial. When growing in deep water the stems can reach a length of 60cm but when on exposed mud Starwort is a prostrate plant with stems seldom reaching 15cm. The leaves can vary from strap-shaped through spoon-shaped to oval dependent on whether they are submerged or aerial. The floating leaves form dense rosettes, sometimes forming extensive mats. The flowers are borne in the leaf axils of the floating leaves and are tiny, without petals. The fruits, which are the only reliable means of precise identification, are also very small (up to 2mm long), and in this species are round with noticeable wings.

Range and habitat: Widespread and common throughout the British Isles and Europe. A common plant of a wide variety of aquatic habitats from medium-flowing rivers to puddles.

Similar species: There are between 6 and 10 species in the region but all are difficult to separate.

MARSH PENNYWORT

Hydrocotyle vulgaris

Characteristics: A low, creeping perennial, rooting at the nodes and often forming mats in damp habitats. The glossy green leaves are held on short to medium length stalks (up to 15cm) and are circular (the stem is at the centre) with shallowly-lobed edges. The flowers are on separate short stalks and are held in a small terminal cluster of 2 to 5 tiny pale pink flowers. The fruits are shaped like a typical member of the carrot or umbellifer family. The flowers are often hard to find.

Range and habitat: Found throughout the British Isles and much of Europe south from Denmark. A fairly common plant of marshes, pond edges, wet woodland rides and bogs, usually on acidic soils, although it is occasionally found in calcareous fens.

Similar species: The circular leaves are similar to Navelwort (see p. 125) but that plant grows on walls and banks and has a distinctive spike of greenish flowers.

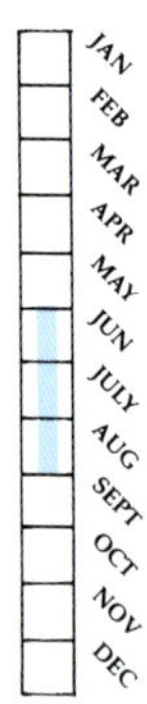

fruit

FOOL'S WATERCRESS

Apium nodiflorum

Characteristics: A largely aquatic or creeping, hairless perennial growing up to 90cm long. The leaves are pinnately lobed with 4 to 6 pairs of bluntly toothed shiny green oval leaflets. The flowers are in shortly stalked uneven umbels and have bracteoles but no bracts. The fruits are oval-shaped.

Range and habitat: Found in England, Wales and Ireland but increasingly rare to the north, including Scotland. Widespread in central and southern Europe. A plant of ditches, ponds and streams, especially in calcareous areas where it can become dominant.

Similar species: This is often confused with Watercress and Lesser Water-parsnip. It is worth checking closely as the latter is poisonous. Watercress has more rounded untoothed leaflets; the flowers are not held in an umbel and develop typical fruit capsules of the cabbage family. Lesser Water-parsnip has dull, more clearly toothed leaflets, usually 5 to 9 pairs on the main leaves. The umbel of flowers has bracts and bracteoles and almost spherical fruits.

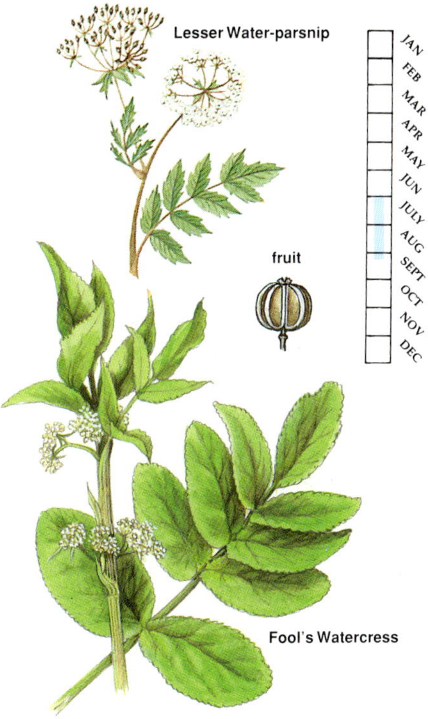

HEMLOCK WATER-DROPWORT

Oenanthe crocata

Characteristics: A large, erect branching perennial, growing up to 150cm, sometimes forming dense stands. The leaves are triangular in outline, up to 30cm long and are 3-4 times pinnate. The stalks form a sheath around the grooved stem. The leaflets are lobed with a tapered base. The umbels of white flowers are held at the top of the plant and the many rays (12 or more) have bracts and bracteoles. The fruit is oblong with two horns (styles) on top. One of the most poisonous plants in the region.

Range and habitat: It has a scattered distribution in the British Isles, being fairly common in southern and western areas. Found widely in southern and western Europe. A plant of pond and stream edges as well as damp woodlands, usually on acid soils.

Similar species: The combination of the large, robust habit and the lobed, oval-shaped leaflets, the many rayed umbel with both bracts and bracteoles should distinguish this plant.

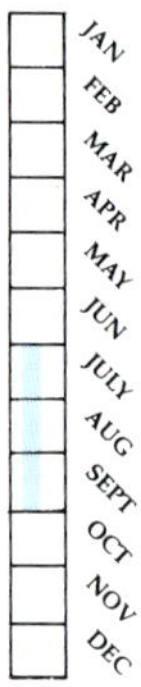

WILD ANGELICA

Angelica sylvestris

Characteristics: A tall, stout-looking perennial with hollow, purplish-coloured stems, growing up to 200cm. The leaves are large and triangular in outline, 2 to 3 times pinnate. The leaflets are oval and pointed with a serrated edge. The leaf stalk has a noticeable channel along the top. The upper leaves are reduced to a large sheathing base with a small protruding leaf; the flower stalk arises from between these upper sheaths and the stem. The pinkish-white flowerheads are many rayed and have a few bracteoles but no bracts. The fruits are oval and flattened.

Range and habitat: Found throughout the British Isles and most of Europe, although rarer in the south. A common plant of damp meadows and pastures, fens, streamsides and open wet woodland.

Similar species: Could be confused with Hogweed (see p. 66) from a distance but that plant has coarser, broader leaf segments and is hairy all over. It also has bracts.

AMPHIBIOUS BISTORT

Polygonum amphibium

Characteristics: An unusual perennial in that it occurs in two distinct forms which can sometimes even be seen on a single plant. The aquatic form is hairless with long-stalked, floating, oblong to lance-shaped leaves with heart-shaped bases. The terrestrial form is downy and often erect (up to 75cm) with short-stalked leaves with rounded bases. The pink flowering spike has a dense leafless terminal cluster of tiny flowers 2-3mm long.

Range and habitat: Found throughout the British Isles and Europe. A common plant of slow-moving rivers and streams, canals, ponds and lakes. The terrestrial form grows along lake and riversides but can also be a weed of arable land.

Similar species: Water Pepper, *Polygonum hydropiper*, can be found in similar habitats but never has the floating leaves; its flower-spike is greenish and the peppery-tasting leaves are tapered at the base. Redshank, *P. persicaria*, typically has black blotches on the leaves which are tapered at the base.

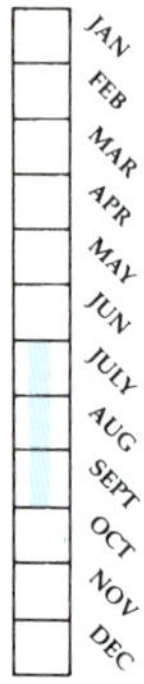

YELLOW LOOSESTRIFE

Lysimachia vulgaris

Characteristics: A tall, downy perennial, growing up to 150cm. The lance-shaped leaves are in opposite pairs or whorls of 3 or 4 up the stem. The upper surface of the leaves is finely dotted with orange or black glands. The yellow flowers are in leafy, branching spikes at the top of the plant. The flowers have a 5-lobed corolla and calyx teeth with orange edges.

Range and habitat: This plant has a scattered distribution throughout most of the British Isles north to central Scotland, although it is far more common in the south. Widespread in Europe. It is a plant of streamsides, fens and lake margins usually on fertile soils.

Similar species: There are two garden plants that might be found naturalised: Dotted Loosestrife, *L. punctata*, which has larger flowers with hairy edges and all-green calyx teeth; Fringed Loosestrife, *L. ciliata*, has rounded corolla-lobes and again lacks the orange margins to the calyx teeth. A rare native of northern Britain, Tufted Loosestrife, *L. thyrsiflora*, has smaller flowers which are held in short, dense clusters.

BOGBEAN

Menyanthes trifoliata

Characteristics: A distinctive, hairless, creeping perennial, usually found in aquatic habitats. When it is growing in water the leaves and flowers are above the water surface. The long-stalked leaves have three large oval leaflets that are held erect. The flowers are in a short flowering spike on the end of a leafless stem, growing up to 30cm tall. The attractive flower has a white 5-lobed corolla, tinged pink on the outside, with a covering inside of white hairs. The fruit is oval and green.

Range and habitat: Widespread throughout the British Isles but only locally common in the south and east. A typical plant of bogs and loch edges in northern and western Britain. Widespread in Europe. It is most characteristic of still waters, bogs and fens on peat.

Similar species: None.

WATER FORGET-ME-NOT

Myosotis scorpioides

Characteristics: A creeping perennial, often forming patches of bright blue flowers by means of its spreading stolons. It grows to a height of 45cm and the stem is covered in a fine coat of adpressed hairs with some upright near the base of the plant. The leaves are narrow and oval to strap-shaped. The flowering spike is leafless. The flowers are clear blue and up to 10mm across with the style just protruding from the corolla. The calyx teeth form equilateral triangles. The stalks when in fruit are one or two times as long as the calyx.

Range and habitat: Widespread throughout the British Isles; scarce in parts of Scotland and Ireland. Found throughout Europe. A common plant of stream edges, marshes and fens on neutral the calcareous soils.

Similar species: Creeping Forget-me-not, *M. secunda*, is a plant of similar habitats on more acid soils. It has slightly smaller flowers, a shorter style and longer calyx teeth. The lower part of the flower spike has leafy bracts.

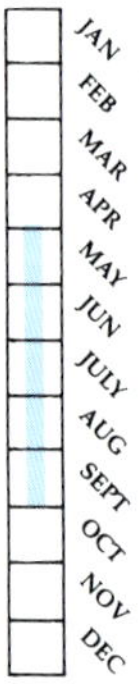

COMFREY

Symphytum officinale

Characteristics: A tall, bristly, branching perennial, growing to 120cm tall. The stems are winged. The large leaves are broadly lance-shaped with the lower ones with stalks, and the upper stalkless, sheathing the stem. The flowers are in nodding, curling clusters. The flowers are bell-shaped with short teeth. The colour varies from creamy white to pink or purple. It is still widely grown as a garden herb.

Range and habitat: Widespread throughout the British Isles but may have been introduced into some areas of Scotland and Ireland. Found throughout Europe. A plant of damp streamsides and marshes.

Similar species: Russian Comfrey, *S. x uplandicum*, is the commonest comfrey and grows on wasteland and along roadsides, avoiding wet ground. It is difficult to separate but usually has dark purple or blue flowers.

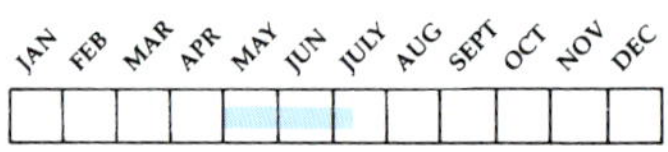

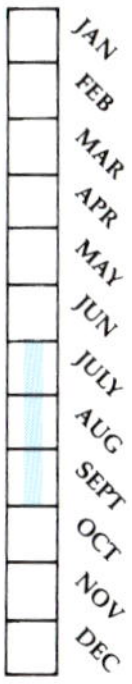

MONKEY FLOWER

Mimulus guttatus

Characteristics: A creeping perennial with upright flowering stems up to 50cm tall. The oval-shaped leaves are in opposite pairs and have shallow teeth. The upper leaves clasp the stem. The flowers are in a leafy spike towards the top of the stem. The bright golden-yellow flower is on a downy stalk and consists of a corolla tube with 2 lips at the opening; the lower one is larger and has 3 lobes; near the throat it has a red-spotted bulge. The upper lip has 2 lobes.

Range and habitat: First introduced to Britain from North America around 1830 and now widely naturalised throughout much of the British Isles except parts of northern Scotland. Also naturalised in Europe. A plant of streams, lake edges and marshes.

Similar species: Blood-drop-emulets, *M. luteus*, is another naturalised plant, this time from Chile. It is found in similar habitats and is best told from the Monkey Flower by its hairless calyx and flower stalk and the large red spots on the lips.

BROOKLIME

Veronica beccabunga

Characteristics: A creeping, hairless perennial with fleshy upright flowering stems, sometimes tinged reddish, to 40cm. The thick, glossy green leaves have short stalks, are in opposite pairs, oval and bluntly toothed. The flowers are in spikes which arise in pairs from opposite leaf axils. The flowers themselves are small (7-8mm across) and blue with 4 lobes. The fruit is round and shorter than the calyx. The young leaves have been used in salads both in Britain and northern Europe and were recommended to prevent scurvy.

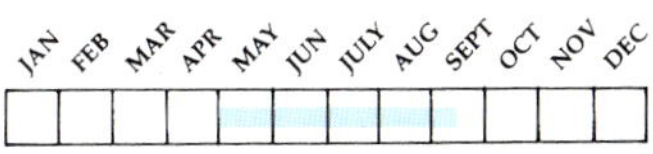

Range and habitat: Widespread throughout the British Isles, except for parts of northern Scotland, where the plant is mostly coastal in its distribution. Found throughout most of Europe. A common plant of stream and pond edges, marshes and fens usually on fertile soils, sometimes forming a carpet on muddy surfaces by means of its creeping stems that root at the nodes.

Similar species: Told from other waterside speedwells by the fleshy, rounded and stalked leaves.

BLUE WATER-SPEEDWELL

Veronica anagallis-aquatica

Characteristics: A fleshy creeping short-lived perennial or annual with upright flowering stems to 30cm tall. The leaves are opposite, lance-shaped, slightly toothed and stalkless. The flower spikes are long and arise in opposite pairs from the leaf axils in the top half of the plant. The 4-lobed flowers are pale blue and 5-6mm across. The fruits are round.

Range and habitat: Widespread throughout the British Isles but only common in central and southern England. Found throughout Europe. A plant of muddy stream and pond edges, marshes and wet meadows.

Similar species: Pink Water-speedwell, *V. catenata*, grows in similar habitats but is more uncommon, being most frequent in south-east England. It has pink rather than pale blue flowers, wider bracts and when in fruit the flower stalk is held at right angles to the stem as opposed to Blue Water-speedwell where it is at a more acute angle.

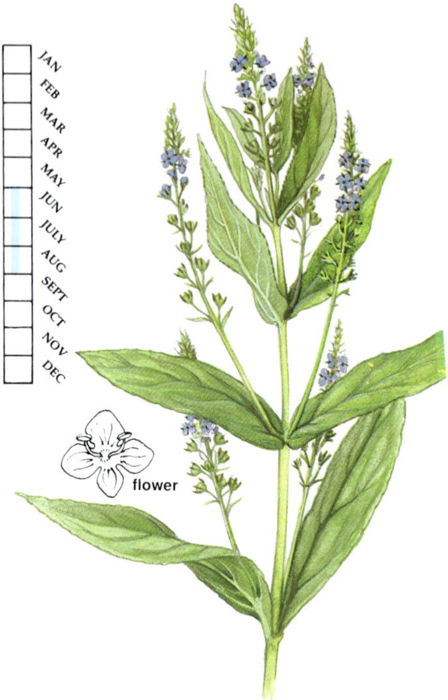

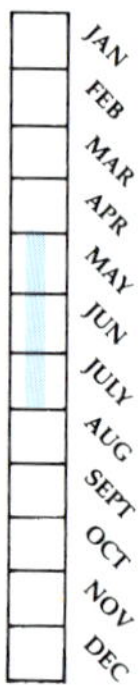

COMMON BUTTERWORT

Pinguicula vulgaris

Characteristics: Distinctive, insectivorous perennial covered in sticky glandular hairs. The narrow, oval, yellowish-green leaves form a flat basal rosette. The upper surface of the leaf is particularly sticky and insects that land on it become trapped whilst the leaf slowly curls up at the edges; eventually enzymes digest the insect. The flower is held on the end of a leafless stalk, up to 15cm tall. It is violet and carried horizontally with a pointed spur at the back and an open mouth with two distinct lips, the upper 2-lobed and the larger lower one with 3 lobes. There is a large white area at the entrance to the mouth.

Range and habitat: Widely distributed throughout the British Isles and Europe but predominately a plant of northern and western areas. It is very rare in lowland England. It is a typical plant of wet flushes in upland areas.

Similar species: Pale Butterwort, *P. lusitanica*, has a distinctly western distribution, has darker green leaves and a smaller, paler flower.

COMMON BLADDERWORT

Utricularia vulgaris

Characteristics: An unusual free-floating, insectivorous perennial. The leaves are roughly oval in outline but are divided into many fine strap-shaped segments. These have a toothed edge with fine bristles. In between the segments are tiny (3mm across) bladders. These have fine bristles at their entrance which when touched by a small animal, such as a water flea, cause the bladder to open and the animal is drawn in with the sudden rush of water. When the plant has absorbed the decayed remains of the animal it expels it as well as the water. The flowers are in a loose spike at the top of a tall, leafless stem, up to 20cm above the water surface. The flower is a golden-yellow, with two lips, the lower one being larger. There is a short, downturned, conical spur.
Range and habitat: Widely distributed throughout the British Isles but nowhere common. Found throughout Europe. A plant of deep peaty pools.
Similar species: There are two other closely related species in the region.

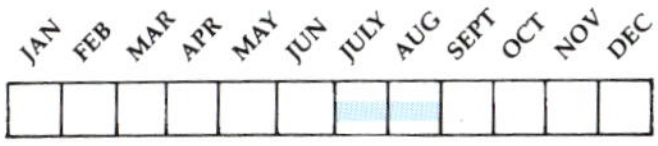

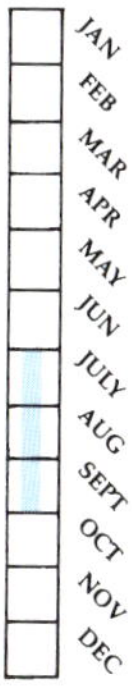

WATER MINT

Mentha aquatica

Characteristics: A strongly-scented, hairy, erect perennial, growing up to 90cm tall. The stems are often a reddish colour. The leaves are short-stalked and oval with a serrated edge, and distinctly mint-scented when bruised. The flowers are in 2 or 3 dense whorls at the top of the plant forming a distinctive lilac-coloured terminal spike, with a few whorls just below. The calyx is hairy and the stamens protrude beyond the 4-lobed corolla.
Range and habitat: The most likely truly wild mint to be encountered. It is widespread throughout the British Isles and most of Europe. A common plant of stream and pond edges, marshes, fens and damp meadows.
Similar species: There are a number of widely naturalised garden species, many of which hybridise with each other making positive identification rather difficult. The other wild mint likely to be found is Corn Mint, *M. arvensis*, which has a less attractive smell and has its whorls of flowers in the leaf axils up the stem but not at the top.

GYPSYWORT

Lycopus europaeus

Characteristics: An erect, branching, hairy perennial, growing up to 100cm. The leaves are variable in size and broadly lance-shaped with pointed tips, rather like a Stinging Nettle. The edges are deeply toothed giving some plants a ragged appearance. The flowers are in tight whorls in the leaf axils. The flower consists of a tiny white corolla (up to 3mm long) with 4 more or less equal lobes, the bottom one of which is dotted with purple spots. The calyx teeth have spines. The plant produces a black dye, with which at one time it was thought gypsies stained themselves, hence the name.

Range and habitat: A widespread plant in southern Britain, rare in Scotland. Found throughout Europe. A common plant of stream and pond edges, marshes, fens and wet woodlands usually on fertile soils.

Similar species: The deeply toothed leaves and whorls of tiny white flowers distinguish it from other members of the mint family.

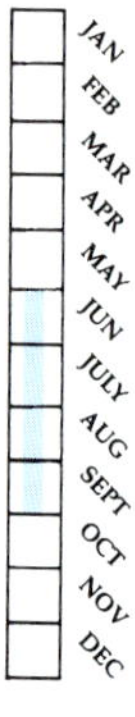

COMMON SKULLCAP

Scutellaria galericulata

Characteristics: An erect, slightly downy perennial, growing to 50cm tall. The opposite leaves are lance-shaped and shortly stalked with shallow teeth. The flowers arise from the leaf axils often singly and typically point in the same direction rather like Common Cow-wheat. The flower itself is deep blue with a long corolla tube, a hooded upper lip and recurved lower lip. The calyx is distinctive with a noticeable scale on the top which is supposed to make the calyx as a whole resemble a Roman skull cap or 'galerum', hence the name.

Range and habitat: Widely distributed in the British Isles but scarce and absent from parts of the north-east and local in Ireland. Found throughout most of Europe. It is a plant of marshy riversides and fens, pond and lake edges and streams; often difficult to find amongst the taller herbs.

Similar species: Lesser Skullcap, *S. minor*, is very like a smaller version of Common Skullcap but has pinkish flowers and the leaves are untoothed.

COMMON VALERIAN

Valeriana officinalis

Characteristics: An erect, robust-looking perennial, growing up to 150cm tall. The opposite leaves are pinnate with shallowly toothed, lance-shaped leaflets. The lower leaves are stalked and can grow to 20cm in length. The flowers form branching umbel-like heads at the top of the plant. The individual pinkish-white flowers are tiny (up to 5mm across) with 5 corolla lobes. The corolla tube is swollen towards the base. The smell of the dried root is supposed to attract cats.

Range and habitat: Found throughout nearly all of the British Isles and Europe, except for the extreme north. A plant of marshes and fens, stream edges and scrub amongst tall dense vegetation, where all but its large panicles of pinkish flowers are almost lost in the herbage.

Similar species: The Marsh Valerian, *V. dioica*, is a smaller plant of wet meadows and fens, usually with white flowers. It can be differentiated by the basal leaves which are oval and undivided; the stem leaves are pinnate.

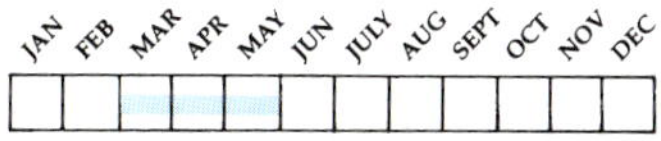

BUTTERBUR

Petasites hybridus

Characteristics: A stout, hairy perennial with creeping rhizomes from which arise separate leaves and flowering stems. The leaves which are typically produced after the plant has flowered are up to 90cm across when fully opened and are broadly heart-shaped and on long stalks. They are green above and felted beneath, looking rather like rhubarb leaves. The flowering spike is leafless but has a series of leaf-like bracts sheathing the stout stem. The pinkish-white flowers are in a dense terminal series of whorls. It is usually dioecious and the male flowers are usually shorter stalked, the female flowers developing into heads of plumed seeds.

Range and habitat: Widespread throughout most of England, Wales and Ireland. Absent from parts of north-east Scotland. The female plant seems most common in northern and central England. Found throughout most of Europe. It is a plant of damp streamsides and wet meadows.

Similar species: Two garden escapes, Giant Butterbur, *P. japonicus*, and White Butterbur, *P. albus*, can be found occasionally. They can be told from the native plant by their white flowerheads. Giant Butterbur has massive leaves that are hairless underneath.

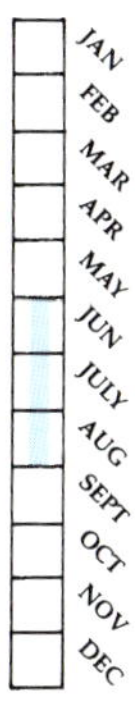

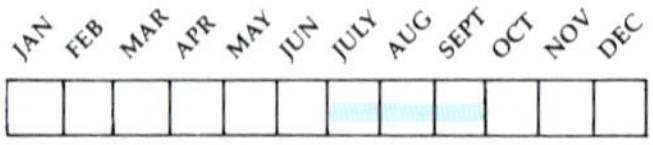

HEMP AGRIMONY

Eupatorium cannibinum

Characteristics: An erect, downy perennial, growing up to 120cm, sometimes forming dense waterside stands. The shortly-stalked leaves are trifoliate with each segment lance-shaped and toothed; the leaves are in opposite pairs up the stem giving the impression of whorls of narrow leaves. The branched upper part of the plant is topped by a series of umbel-like dense clusters of pinkish flowerheads. Each flowerhead is made up of only 5 to 6 tubular florets each with a long, forked style; the flowerhead is surrounded by purple-tipped bracts. The seed has a pappus of white hairs. The flowers are attractive to butterflies and moths.

Range and habitat: Widespread in the British Isles but rarer in Scotland where it is mainly a coastal plant. Found throughout Europe. A typical plant of stream and pond edges, marshes and fens, also damp woodland rides.

Similar species: Could be confused with Common Valerian at first glance but the leaves are trifoliate.

MARSH THISTLE

Cirsium palustre

Characteristics: An erect, hairy biennial with a very spiny winged stem, growing up to 150cm or more. The leaves are dark green, narrow, lance-shaped and pinnately lobed; the edges are covered with dark-tipped spines. The flowerheads are in clusters at the top of the main stem and the side branches. They are reddish-purple (sometimes white) with spiny, purplish bracts. The seed has a dirty-white feathery pappus. The numerous flowerheads are attractive to a wide range of insects.

Range and habitat: Found throughout the British Isles and Europe. A common plant of a wide range of wet habitats from marshes and fens to damp meadows and woodland rides.

Similar species: Told from the Spear Thistle by the winged stems and from Creeping Thistle by the flower colour and the hairy surface to the leaves. Welted Thistle, *Carduus crispus*, is more branched and greener with cottony bracts.

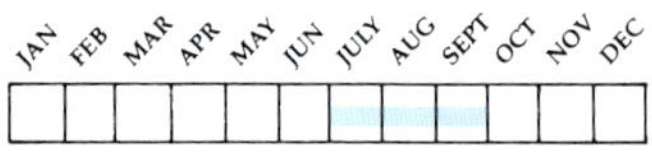

COMMON WATER-PLANTAIN

Alisma plantago-aquatica

Characteristics: An erect, hairless, aquatic perennial, growing up to 100cm. The leaves are in a semi-erect basal rosette and are long stalked, oval to lance-shaped, rounded at the base, with clear parallel veins rather like a plantain, hence its name. The numerous flowers are in a series of decreasing, branched whorls at the top of a leafless stem. The flowers themselves are 3-petalled and pale pink with 3 blunt, green sepals. The flowers open in the afternoon and early evening.

Range and habitat: Found throughout most of the British Isles, although rare and absent in parts of northern Scotland. Found throughout Europe. A fairly common plant of muddy edges of lakes, ponds, streams and slow-flowing rivers.

Similar species: Narrow-leaved Water-plantain, *A. lanceolatum*, is found in similar habitats but is more confined to the south and rarer. It has narrower leaves that taper into the stem and darker flowers which open in the morning.

ARROWHEAD

Sagittaria sagittifolia

Characteristics: An erect, hairless aquatic perennial, overwintering by means of a submerged bud, growing up to 90cm. The leaves vary depending on the water flow. In more sluggish conditions there are many aerial leaves which are held clear of the water surface on long stalks and have a striking arrow-shape with large backward pointing lobes. In faster waters there are many submerged strap-like leaves. There are also floating leaves which are oval, rather like a pondweed. The whorls of flowers are held clear of the water on tall leafless stalks. The white flowers have 3 petals with a purple spot at the base. The male flowers are at the top, the female ones below.

Range and habitat: Mainly confined to England, rare in parts of Wales and Ireland, absent from Scotland. Widespread in Europe. A locally frequent plant of unpolluted lake margins, canals, and slow-flowing rivers.

Similar species: Where there are only strap-shaped leaves, could be confused with Bur-reed, *Sparganium emersum*.

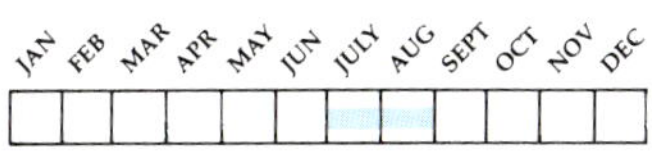

CANADIAN PONDWEED

Elodea canadensis

Characteristics: A submerged, hairless perennial with long stems (usually up to 100cm but can be longer), often forming dense underwater masses. The whole plant is a translucent, dark green colour with strap-shaped leaves in close whorls of 3 along the stem. The flowers are carried singly on long, thread-like stalks that carry them to the surface. The plant is dioecious and in Britain only the female is usual with 3 pale petals and sepals and 3 reddish styles. The plant was first introduced into Europe in the first half of the 19th Century from North America. It spread so rapidly along our rivers and canals that it became a threat to navigation. A minister was even appointed in the 1860s to control the problem. Luckily its natural vigour has decreased and it is no longer a threat.

Range and habitat: Found in most rivers, ponds, canals and dykes north to southern Scotland. Naturalised throughout most of Europe.

Similar species: *Elodea nuttallii* has more pointed and recurved leaves.

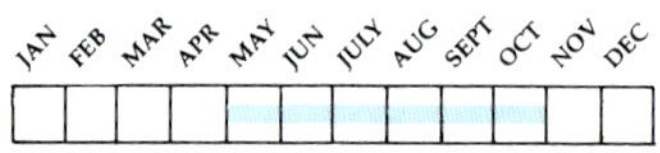

BROAD-LEAVED PONDWEED

Potamogeton natans

Characteristics: A submerged and floating perennial with long stalks up to 2m long. The floating leaves are oval in shape, dark green and leathery with distinct parallel veins along the length. The submerged leaves are strap-shaped. The leaf stipules are long and pointed enclosing the stem. The flowers are in a cylindrical spike held on a long stalk just above the surface of the water.

Range and habitat: Found throughout the British Isles and Europe. A common plant of slow-flowing rivers.

Similar species: There are 21 species of pondweed in Britain and although they vary considerably in their characters they are not an easy group to identify because individual plants differ according to the environment in which they are growing, a problem that is compounded by the fact that some hybridise. A widespread and common species that is worth looking out for in more acid waters is the Curled Pondweed, *P. crispus,* which has long, strap-like, wavy leaves.

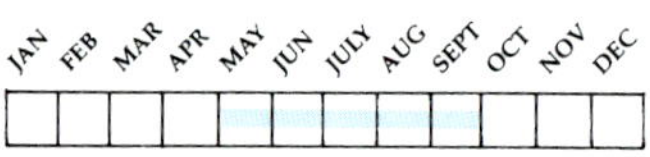

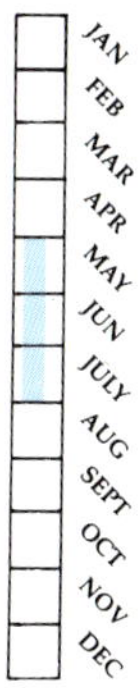

YELLOW FLAG

Iris pseudocorus

Characteristics: An attractive, erect perennial, growing up to 150cm, sometimes forming dense stands. The leaves are upright, flat and sword-shaped. The flowering stalk is branched near the top and typically as high as the leaves. The large showy, yellow flowers are up to 10cm across with 3 large down-curved outer petals and 3 more erect inner ones, called standards. In between these are the petal-like stigmas. In fruit the plant has large green, oval-shaped pods which split to reveal brown seeds.

Range and habitat: Widely distributed throughout most of the British Isles and Europe. A common plant of riversides, pond and lake edges and marshes usually on fertile soils.

Similar species: Unmistakable in flower, the leaves could be confused with Stinking Iris, *I. foetidissima*, a plant of well-drained basic soils in southern Britain. However, if you bruise the leaf it smells strongly of roast beef. The erect leaves of bur-reeds can also look similar but they are 3-sided.

COMMON DUCKWEED

Lemna minor

Characteristics: A curious aquatic plant which consists primarily of a green, circular, floating frond or thallus, 1.5-4mm across. The minute flowers are only produced occasionally and the plant typically spreads by vegetative buds, sometimes completely covering still water with a bright green mantle. A single root hangs down from the plant.

Range and habitat: Found commonly throughout the British Isles, although less frequent in parts of northern Scotland. Widespread and common in Europe. This plant is found in every continent except the Antarctic. A plant of slow-flowing rivers and ditches as well as pools and ponds.

Similar species: There are 5 other species of duckweed in the region. Greater Duckweed, *L. polyrhiza,* is larger (5-8mm across) and purplish below, with several roots. Ivy-leaved Duckweed, *L. trisulca,* is submerged, forming semi-transparent branching colonies, the stalks attaching to each other at right angles.

HEATHS, MOORS AND MOUNTAINS

These three apparently different habitats have certain characteristics in common in that the soils are usually poor and acidic, often leached of nutrients by high rainfall. These conditions are ripe for colonisation by members of the Heath family and its most abundant member, Ling, is often a dominant plant of these habitats, forming a dense low shrub layer across many miles of upland moors and large areas of heaths.

Heaths are lowland habitats created initially by the removal of the woodland over areas of poor gravelly soils and kept open by grazing and fires. In many areas, the practice of grazing has ceased and the remaining open heaths are threatened by encroachment from scrub and development. Although not as rich in species as some other habitats, they have their own distinctive plant communities, including flowers such as the Bell Heather and Cross-leaved Heath which sometimes form a complex pattern amongst the Ling, picking out the drier and wetter parts of the land. In the wetter areas, also look out for the sundews which make up for the deficiency in the soil nutrients by catching insects on their sticky leaves.

The upland moors and mountain areas can be dominated by vast sweeps of Ling with few other plant other than tough grasses in places that have been over-grazed. Where there are wet flushes or rocky overhangs out of the reach of nibbling sheep, other plants can survive. It is in these places, particularly if the underlying rocks are base-rich, that some of the sought after alpine plants such as Mountain Avens and Yellow Marsh Saxifrage can be found.

Ponies grazing moorland in Dartmoor amidst a mosaic of Western Gorse, Heather, Bell Heather and Bracken.

GORSE

Ulex europaeus

Characteristics: A robust, spiny, densely branching shrub sometimes forming impenetrable thickets, growing up to 200cm. The whole plant is covered in large green spines which are furrowed and branching. The large, pea-like yellow flowers often form dense clusters on the upper branches. Although Gorse can be seen in flower in almost any month of the year, it is typically at its best in early spring. The hairy pods explode when they are ripe, scattering the seeds.

Range and habitat: Widespread and common throughout the British Isles; less common in intensively farmed areas. In Europe it is more restricted and is found primarily along the western seaboard. A plant of rough grassland and heaths on acid soils, it can be invasive after soil disturbance.

Similar species: Western Gorse, *U. gallii*, has a distinctly western distribution and is usually smaller than Gorse and the calyx is less hairy and 10-13mm long. Usually flowers in the late summer and autumn.

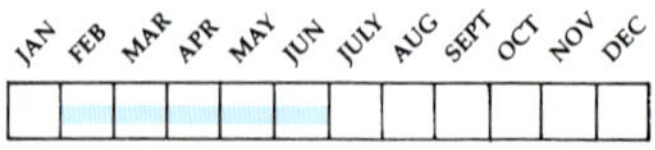

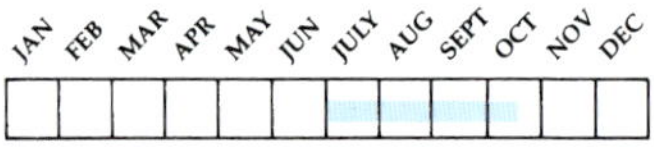

DWARF GORSE

Ulex minor

Characteristics: A smaller version of Gorse, often creeping and seldom growing above 100cm tall. The spines are less noticeably furrowed than Gorse and up to 1cm long. The yellow pea-like flowers are up to 10mm long and the calyx is less hairy than Gorse, 6-9.5mm long. The wings on the flower are shorter or the same length as the keel.

Range and habitat: Restricted in Britain to south-east England. Also occurs in scattered localities in the Midlands and North. Found in western Europe only. A plant of heaths and acid grasslands.

Similar species: Told from the two gorse species described above by the weaker low-growing stems and smaller spines and flowers. The distribution rarely overlaps with Western Gorse. Typically it is in full flower in the late summer and autumn when Gorse will have few flowers.

MOUNTAIN AVENS

Dryas octopetela

Characteristics: A creeping, evergreen shrub, growing up to 8cm tall. The numerous leaves are dark green above and white and downy below. The edges are lobed giving them the appearance of a small oak leaves. The flowers are carried singly above the leaves on long, leafless stalks. The flower itself has 8 white petals with approximately 20 golden stamens. The fruits have long feathery styles.

Range and habitat: An alpine species confined to a few high peaks in the British Isles. Most likely to be found in the mountains of the north of Scotland. Interestingly it is found at sea level in certain parts of the north Scottish coast and in the Burren in western Ireland. It is a plant of basic rocks so is most likely to be found on exposed limestones and mica-schists.

Similar species: None

ROUND-LEAVED SUNDEW

Drosera rotundifolia

Characteristics: A low-growing insectivorous perennial; flower-stalk up to 25cm tall. The leaves are long-stalked and round forming a low rosette. They are covered with red sticky hairs, which are longer towards the edge of the leaf and tipped with a sticky fluid. When a small insect lands on the leaf it immediately becomes trapped by the sticky hairs, the leaf then gradually rolls up and the enzymes from the hairs breakdown the insect so that the nutrients can be absorbed by the leaf. The leafless, upright, flowering spike arises from the centre of the rosette. The white, six-petalled flowers seldom fully open and the flowers are usually self-pollinated.

Range and habitat: Widespread throughout the British Isles but only locally common in intensively farmed areas. Found throughout northern and central Europe. A plant of wet acid habitats, most typically found in *Sphagnum* bogs.

Similar species: The two less common species have narrower leaves.

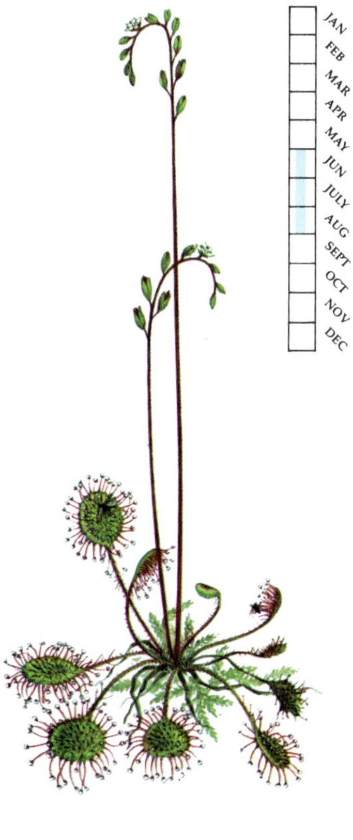

YELLOW MOUNTAIN SAXIFRAGE

Saxifraga azioides

Characteristics: An attractive, low-growing perennial, up to 20cm tall. The leaves are stalkless, pointed and strap-shaped, sometimes forming a dense mass on the non-flowering shoots. The flowers are in a loose cluster. The oval petals are yellow spotted with red; the anthers are also red.

Range and habitat: A locally common plant of uplands in the north of England, Scotland and Ireland. Absent from Wales. It is a good indicator of limestone rocks and flushes, being most typical of mountain streamsides and wet ground.

Similar species: The very rare Yellow Marsh Saxifrage, *Saxifraga hirculus*, is found in a few lime-rich upland areas in northern and western Britain. It has stalked leaves and typically, solitary flowers.

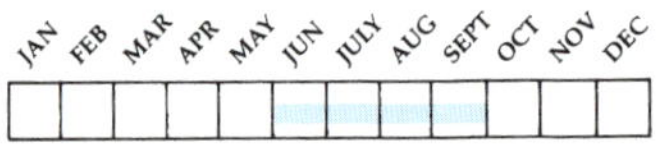

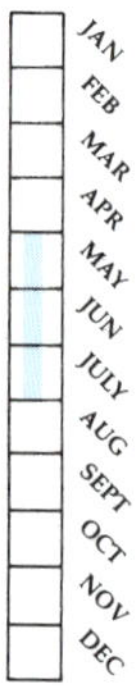

BEARBERRY

Arctostaphylos uva-ursi

Characteristics: A prostrate, evergreen shrub. The alternate leaves are oval with blunt tips and smooth edges. They are thick and dark green with lighter veins, paler beneath. The flowers are in dense clusters and are bell-shaped to globular, white flushed pink. The fruit is a red, shiny berry.

Range and habitat: Found throughout the Scottish Highlands and also scattered upland localities south to Derbyshire and also north-west Ireland. Locally common in Europe. A plant of exposed banks and scree slopes in upland areas, often found on steep open banks beside roads and trackways.

Similar species: Black Bearberry, *A. alpinus*, is a rare plant of high mountains and moors. It has toothed, deciduous leaves and black berries. Cowberry also has red berries but has white bell-shaped flowers with up-turned lobes.

HEATHER, LING

Calluna vulgaris

Characteristics: A familiar evergreen, low-growing shrub which can dominate large areas. Heather has numerous twisting branches and typically grows up to 60cm tall. The numerous small leaves are in pairs up the main stems and are unstalked with 2 pointed lobes at the base. The leaves on non-flowering shoots are densely packed in 4 rows. The flower spikes are up to 15cm long, usually at the end of the main branches and on side-shoots. The numerous flowers are a pale purple colour and are 4-lobed and tiny (up to 4mm).

Range and habitat: Widespread and common throughout the British Isles and much of Europe, though most common in the west. A typical plant of acid, leached soils and peatlands, in both upland and lowland regions often becoming dominant over large areas. Large areas of lowland Heather have been lost to agricultural improvements, forestry and development.

Similar species: Cross-leaved Heath and Bell Heather can be confused.

CROSS-LEAVED HEATH

Erica tetralix

Characteristics: A low-growing evergreen shrub with numerous, semi-erect branches. The stems and leaves are covered in glandular hairs. The leaves are in whorls of 4, clearly spaced up the stems. The leaves themselves are strap-shaped, with the edges almost curled under up to the middle and grey-green. The rose-pink drooping flowers are in a tight one-sided terminal cluster and are globular with very short lobes at the mouth.

Range and habitat: Found throughout most of the British Isles and western Europe. A plant of wet heaths, moors and bogs on acid peaty soils where it can be dominant. Seldom found outside these habitats so absent from area of intensive farming and dry basic soils.

Similar species: Can be confused with the other heathers but look for the whorls of 4, greyish leaves and the drooping pinkish flowers.

BELL HEATHER

Erica cinerea

Characteristics: A low-growing evergreen shrub with numerous semi-erect branches with many short leafy sideshoots. The leaves are in whorls of 3, dark green and hairless. The flowers are in a short terminal spike and are deep purple. The corolla is globular with short upturned lobes at the mouth.

Range and habitat: Widespread throughout the British Isles but scarce or absent from highly cultivated areas, especially the Midlands. Found in western Europe only. A plant of dry, acid soils usually with other heath species, sometimes dominant. Often forms a mosaic with Cross-leaved Heath, one picking out the dryer areas and the other the boggy parts.

Similar species: Dorset Heath, *E. ciliaris,* also has leaves in whorls of 3 but tends to be taller with flowers in a distinct deep pink spike. Very locally abundant in south-western England, western France and Spain.

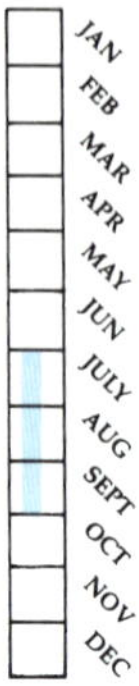

BILBERRY

Vaccinium myrtillus

Characteristics: A low, branching, deciduous shrub, growing up to 60cm. The stems are green and angled. The alternate leaves are 1-3cm long, bright green, oval-shaped and finely toothed. The flowers arise singly or in pairs from the leaf axils and are drooping, globular and a dull pink in colour. The fruits are edible and black, at first with a plum-like bloom.

Range and habitat: Found throughout most of the British Isles but less common and absent from areas of central and south-eastern England. Widespread in Europe. A plant of dry acid soils, often in association with heathers. Sometimes forms an important part of the undershrub layer in woods.

Similar species: Bog Bilberry, *V. uliginosum*, has round, brown twigs and waxy grey, untoothed leaves. Also has paler flowers. It is a local upland plant. Cowberry, *V. vitis-idaea,* is a locally common evergreen shrub of upland moors and woods. It has glossy green leaves, white, bell-shaped flowers with recurved lobes and a bright red berry.

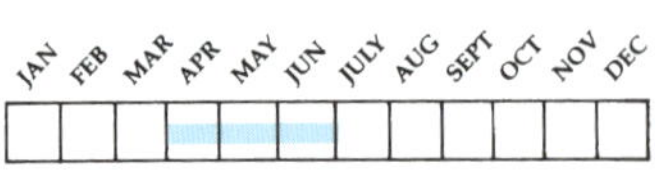

CROWBERRY

Empetrum nigrum

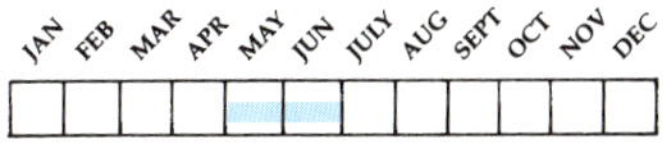

Characteristics: A low-growing, sometimes mat-forming (up to 45cm tall), evergreen shrub, looking rather like a heather species but in fact in a different family. The leaves are alternate and strap-shaped, glossy green with inrolled margins. The tiny flowers are dioecious, with the male and female flowers on separate plants. The smaller male flowers have 3 long stamens. Both types of flowers have 6 pink sepals. The fruit is a berry which ripens through pink and purple to black. It is apparently a favourite food of the grouse.
Range and habitat: Found throughout northern and western Britain. Found widely in northern and central Europe. A sometimes abundant plant of upland moors and mountains on drier peaty soils.
Similar species: Told from heather species by the alternate leaves and 6-lobed sepals. There are 2 subspecies of Crowberry, with subspecies *hermaphroditum* found in higher altitudes.

COMMON DODDER

Cuscuta epithymum

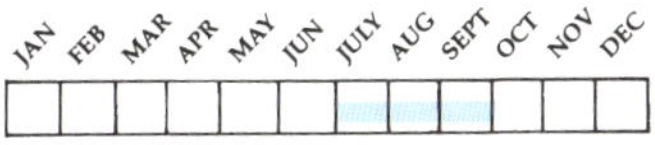

Characteristics: An unusual parasitic annual, that has twining stems attached to the host plant. It can be so vigorous that it can blanket out the host plant from view and eventually kill it. The stems are very thin and red and are attached to the host plant by suckers, through which the plant draws its nutrients. The small pink flowers are in dense stalkless clusters. The flowers are bell-shaped with a darker, lobed calyx. Formerly a hated arable weed species.
Range and habitat: Found locally in southern England. Widespread in central Europe. Usually parasitic on members of the pea-family, particularly Gorse, also on Heather, therefore most likely to be found on lowland heaths.
Similar species: Greater Dodder, is similar but larger and parasitic on Nettle and occasionally on Hop. It is now a rare and declining plant in Britain. Also found in Europe.

LOUSEWORT
Pedicularis sylvatica

Characteristics: A low-growing, hairless semi-parasitic perennial, up to 25cm tall. The leaves are spreading, pinnate and toothed, oblong in outline, looking rather fern-like. The flowers are in a terminal cluster, often with only a few flowers, and have a large tubular calyx which becomes inflated in fruit. The rose-pink corolla has a hooded upper lip with 2 small teeth and a 3-lobed spreading lower lip. The name is possibly derived from an association with this plant and poor damp pasture where liver fluke would have been present.
Range and habitat: Found throughout the British Isles in suitable habitat. Widespread in western and central Europe. A plant of damp acid grassland, heaths, bogs and marshes.
Similar species: Marsh Lousewort, *P. palustris,* is similar but typically much taller growing in wetter habitats, including calcareous fens as well as bogs. The upper lip of this species has 4 teeth rather than 2.

HEATH BEDSTRAW
Galium saxatile

Characteristics: A low-growing perennial, up to 20cm, sometimes forming dense white-flowered mats. The stems are 4-angled but without spines. The leaves are in whorls of 6-8 and are narrowly ovate with spines on the leaf edge pointing forward; the tip of the leaf also has a spine. The tiny white flowers are in dense short clusters arising from leaf axils up the stem. The round fruits are hairless but with a warty surface.
Range and habitat: Found throughout the British Isles and central and western Europe. A common plant of heaths and grassland, moors and woodland rides, almost always on dry acid soils.
Similar species: Only other white-flowered bedstraw with smooth stems and forward-pointing prickles on the leaves is Hedge Bedstraw (see p. 40); this is far more upright and robust looking with larger, broader leaves and flowers in a showy terminal cluster.

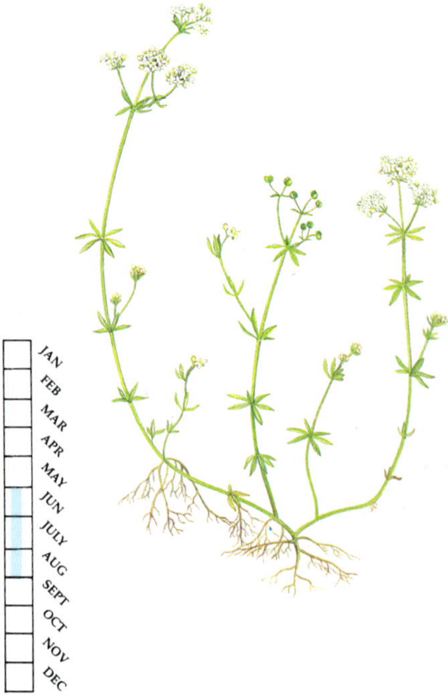

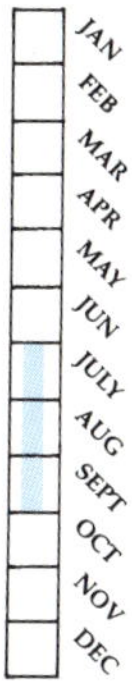

BOG ASPHODEL

Narthecium ossifragum

Characteristics: An attractive, hairless upright perennial, up to 40cm.This member of the lily family provides a bright splash of colour to bogs and wet heaths in mid-summer, often forming large patches by means of its creeping rhizomes. The basal leaves are often curved and are flattened and sword-shaped. The leaves on the flowering stem are smaller and sheathing. The flower are in a terminal flowering spike. The flower consists of 6 narrow, pointed yellow petals with 6 erect stamens covered with golden-yellow hairs with orange anthers. As the plant matures it becomes an orange colour.
Range and habitat: A widespread and sometimes abundant plant in suitable habitat throughout the British Isles but scarce or absent in areas of central and south-eastern England. Found in western Europe. A plant of wet heaths, moors and bogs.
Similar species: None.

HEATH SPOTTED ORCHID

Dactylorhiza maculata

Characteristics: A variable orchid growing up to 50cm. The leaves are narrow lance-shaped and pointed with dark spots. The flowerhead is densely packed and conical. The overall colour of the flowers varies from white through pink to purple often within the same site. The three outer sepals are spreading with the two upper petals forming a hood. The lip has a broadly U-shaped pattern of crimson dots and dashes and has three lobes, the centre one being smaller than the outer two.
Range and habitat: Widespread throughout the British Isles and northern and central Europe where there is suitable habitat. A fairly common plant of acid grassland, heaths, moors and bogs.
Similar species: The Common Spotted Orchid (see p. 85) is very similar but has broader blunt-tipped lower leaves and the lip has three equal-sized lobes with the centre one dagger-shaped.

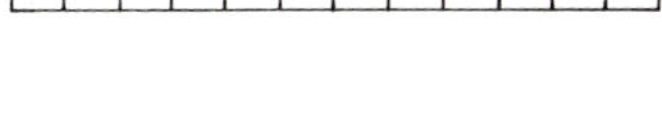

COASTS

Although the flowering plants have not colonised the marine environment in the way that seaweeds have, they have managed to adapt to the wide variety of niches that can be found along the coast, from brackish lagoons and saltmarshes to sheer cliff edges and shingle beaches.

Estuaries, although at first glance appearing to be empty 'waste-lands', are extremely rich habitats as the sheltered, muddy flats are supplied with a double dose of nutrients every day from the sediments deposited by the rivers and tides. Where the mud is consolidated, saltmarsh plants can take a foothold with pioneer species able to take a regular dosing of sea water at the outer edges; these include Glasswort and cord-grasses. On slightly higher ground, plants such as Sea-lavender and Sea Aster can become established, sometimes forming extensive carpets. The taller Sea-purslane is a shrub that grows along the edges of creeks, helping to bind the mud.

Exposed rocky shores are less hospitable to plants than estuaries, but out of the reach of the crashing waves the surface is quickly colonised by plants such as Sea and Buck's-horn Plantains and the colourful pink Thrift. This last plant, together with Sea Campion, can cover the cliff tops in hummocky masses, turning the cliffs into a riot of colour in June.

Shingle beaches must represent one of the most inhospitable habitats for plants, with the waves constantly throwing up the pebbles on the lower shore and the contours changing after each storm. However, above the high spring tide mark a number of plants, such as the tall Yellow Horned-poppy, with its long, curving, seed pods, and Biting Stonecrop, are able to successfully colonise the shingle.

Sand dunes are an important habitat for wildlife and their very existence is due to the binding quality of plants such as Marram Grass and Lyme Grass, which allow the sand dunes to build up. Look out for tiny annuals like the Common Stork's-bill and other plants of open, unstable habitats.

Yellow Horned-poppy on shingle.

YELLOW HORNED-POPPY

Glaucium flavum

Characteristics: An erect, waxy-grey, branching coastal perennial, up to 90cm tall, which can survive in apparently soilless situations by means of a long tap-root. All parts of the plant are poisonous and if it is cut it oozes a yellow latex. The basal leaves are in a rosette and are hairy and pinnately lobed. The stem leaves are also lobed but smaller. The flower is large (up to 9cm across), with hairy sepals and 4, large, yellow petals. The distinctive, curved seed pod grows up to 30cm.
Range and habitat: It is found along the coast north to Scotland on the west coast but only as far as Lincolnshire on the east coast. Found in southern and western Europe as far north as southern Scandinavia. A plant of shingle and sand dunes, and other well-drained coastal habitats.
Similar species: The only other yellow-flowered poppy is the Welsh Poppy, *Meconopsis cambrica*, which is smaller with an oval-shaped seed pod (up to 3cm); a local plant of western hillsides and a garden escape.

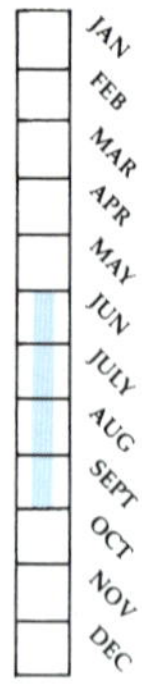

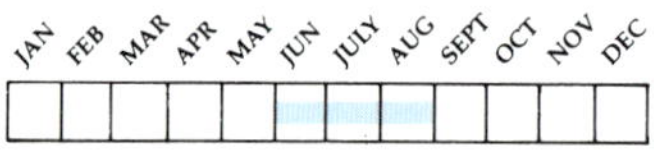

SEA CAMPION

Silene maritima

Characteristics: A low-growing, maritime perennial, up to 25cm tall. Often forms a dense cushion of non-flowering shoots topped by flowering ones. The leaves are in pairs and are narrow, pointed and distinctly waxy. The flowers are usually held solitarily, erect and are up to 25cm across. The flower has 5, white, notched petals and has a cylindrical calyx tube.
Range and habitat: Found all along the coasts of the British Isles, where it can be abundant, sometimes forming dense white carpets of flowers. Widespread along the Atlantic seaboard from Spain to Norway. A plant of shingle, cliff tops and rocky ground. Occasionally found in mountain scree slopes.
Similar species: Bladder Campion (see p. 133) is similar but has a rounder calyx and drooping flowers. Leaves are thinner and less waxy. Moss Campion, *S. acaulis*, is a mountain plant of rocky ground. It forms low compact cushions of tiny leaves and has pink flowers.

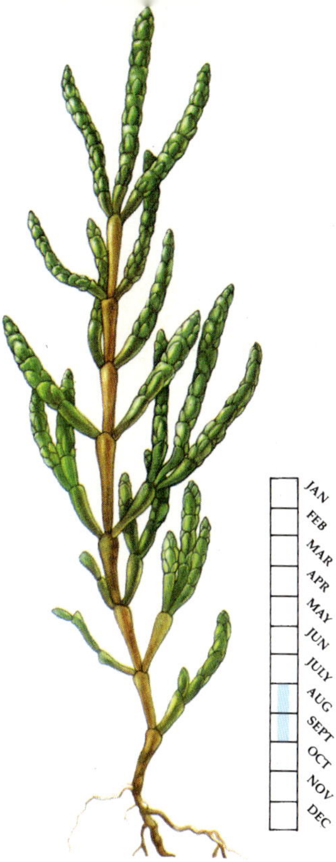

PERENNIAL GLASSWORT

Salicornia perennis

Characteristics: The glassworts are a group of succulent maritime plants that can be very confusing to identify. Perennial Glasswort is fairly distinctive as it has creeping woody stems, up to 1m long, from which arise fleshy, jointed shoots up to 20cm tall, with opposite branches, short or almost absent in some specimens. The swollen segments are in fact leaf sheaths and the leaves are reduced to triangular scales at the junctions. The minute flowers, in groups of 3, are hardly visible and are usually detected by the presence of 2 stamens along the junctions towards the tips. The plant starts off a green colour but during autumn it turns yellow and eventually orange. It is also known as Marsh Samphire and is still collected in some regions for pickling.
Range and habitat: Chiefly found along the south and east coasts with small populations in Wales. Widespread along the Atlantic coast southwards from France. A plant of saltmarshes of the middle shore, sometimes forming extensive colonies.

SEA PURSLANE

Halimone portulacoides

Characteristics: A low, branching maritime shrub, growing up to 80cm. The leaves are mostly opposite and elliptical, covered with minute grey scales giving the plant a silvery or 'mealy' appearance. The flowers are in dense spikes with separate male and female flowers. The flowers are tiny and are yellowish-green; the female has no sepals or petals and consists of a pair of styles protruding from a pair of bracteoles, the male has 5 stamens.
Range and habitat: Widespread around the British coast from central Scotland southwards; also on the east coast of Ireland. Found in Europe from Denmark southwards. A characteristic plant of saltmarshes along the upper margins in estuaries and sheltered coasts. Often forming extensive communities along the edges of creeks and gullies.
Similar species: None.

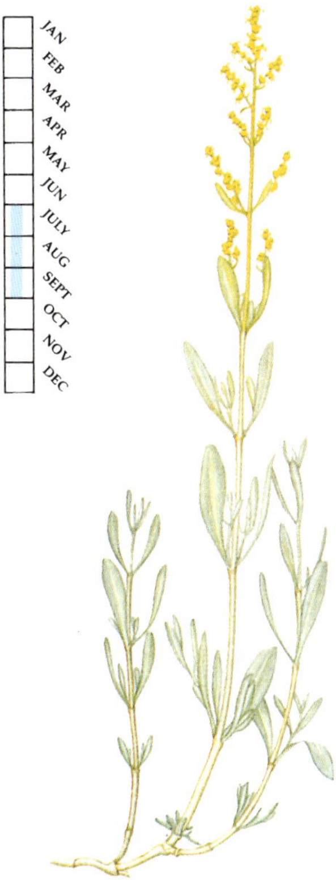

COMMON STORK'S-BILL

Erodium cicutarium

Characteristics: A variable but usually sticky, hairy, low-growing annual, up to 30cm tall. The leaves are 2-pinnate and feathery. The flowers are on long stalks and are in a loose terminal cluster. The flowers have rose-pink oval petals which often drop within a few hours of flowering. The seed capsule is long and pointed like the closely related crane's-bills but the segments instead of curling up twist into a spiral with the seed still attached.

Range and habitat: Found throughout most of the British Isles and Europe. A plant of dry sandy habitats, particularly coastal sand dunes but also found on inland heaths and open sandy grasslands.

Similar species: Sea Stork's-bill, *E. maritimum,* is a local species of southern and western coastal dunes. It has lobed rather than pinnate leaves. Musk Stork's-bill, *E. moschatum,* is another local coastal species; it has blunt rather than pointed stipules.

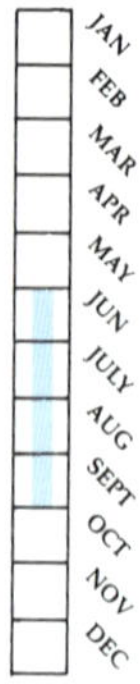

BITING STONECROP

Sedum acre

Characteristics: A low-growing, succulent evergreen perennial, up to 10cm tall. It has creeping stems forming dense mats, with many upright flowering and non-flowering shoots. The tiny yellowish-green leaves (3-5mm), oval and swollen, overlap each other, often hiding the stem near the base. The golden-yellow, star-like flowers (up to 12mm across) are in loose clusters at the ends of the main branches. The leaves have a peppery, acrid taste, hence its names Biting Stonecrop and Wall Pepper.

Range and habitat: Found throughout the British Isles, except for the far north of Scotland. Throughout Europe. A common plant of sand dunes, shingle, walls and open grassland.

Similar species: Reflexed Stonecrop, *S. reflexum,* also has yellow flowers in a dense flat-topped head; the leaves are often held away from the stem.

NAVELWORT

Umbilicus rupestris

Characteristics: A distinctive, erect hairless perennial, growing up to 40cm tall. The fleshy pale leaves, which mostly arise from the base, are circular (up to 7cm across) with a central depression above the junction with the long stalk. The edge has shallow wavy teeth. The flowers are held in an upright spike and consist of many drooping, bell-shaped whitish-green flowers. The round leaves have given the plant many local names, such as Wall Pennywort, Penny Pies and Penny Plates, although it is thought that the name refers to the old silver penny and not the modern copper one.

Range and habitat: Most common in the south-west of England and Wales but found as far north as Scotland and in scattered localities across to eastern England. It also has a south-western distribution in Europe. A plant of rock crevices, old walls and hedgebanks, particularly close to the sea.

Similar species: None.

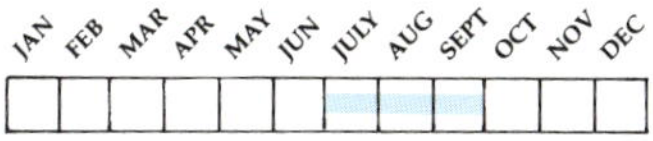

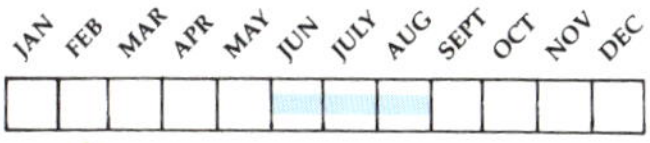

FENNEL

Foeniculum vulgare

Characteristics: A robust, erect hairless perennial member of the carrot family, growing up to 130cm tall. The leaves are a waxy green and feathery with the leaflets divided into many very narrow segments. The leaf-bases form large sheaths. The many-rayed umbels of yellow flowers are up to 8cm across. There are typically no bracts or bracteoles. The fruits are oval-shaped and ribbed. The plant smells strongly when bruised.

Range and habitat: Found along much of the coast around England and Wales; rarer in Scotland and Ireland. A native of the Mediterranean, it has been widely naturalised throughout Europe. It is typically found along cliff edges, tracksides and waste ground near the sea; also more rarely inland.

Similar species: The combination of the finely-divided bushy, blue-grey leaves and yellow umbels is very distinctive. The other large seaside umbellifer with yellow flowers is Alexanders, *Smyrnium olusatrum*, which has leaflets divided into three broad, stalked lobes.

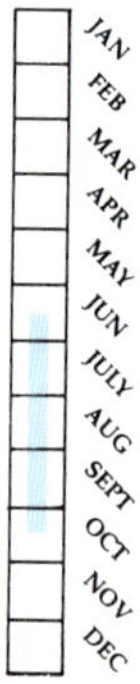

COMMON SEA-LAVENDER

Limonium vulgare

Characteristics: A hairless, upright maritime perennial (up to 30cm tall), with a creeping woody rootstock, often forming extensive colonies. The leaves are in a basal rosette and are semi-erect and lance-shaped with a spine at the tip. The flowers are in flat-topped, dense, erect clusters along the tops of the leafless branching stems.The flowers are a purplish lavender colour with 5 petals and a persistent pale purple calyx.

Range and habitat: Found around the coast of Britain north to central Scotland. Absent from Ireland. Found along the coast in western and southern Europe. A plant of saltmarshes, where it can be dominant forming extensive carpets of flowers.

Similar species: There are several very similar species. Lax-flowered Sea-lavender, *L. humile,* is a more local plant of saltmarshes with the flower stalks branching lower down and narrower leaves. The flower clusters are not so compact. There is also a species which grows on rocks, *L. binoversum.*

THRIFT

Armeria maritima

Characteristics: Low-growing, attractive perennials growing from a woody rootstock, sometimes forming large carpets. The numerous single-veined, strap-shaped leaves form a cushion-like basal rosette. The pink flowers are in a dense rounded terminal head on leafless stalks up to 30cm tall. A papery sheath extends below the flowerhead for 2-3cm. The small flowers are up to 8mm across and have 5 petals and a hairy calyx. The large bracts persist in fruit.

Range and habitat: Widespread in the British Isles and western Europe. A common and sometimes abundant plant of saltmarshes and clifftops. Also occurs as a mountain plant in the north and west where it is found on scree slopes.

Similar species: Jersey Thrift, *A. alliacea,* is a local plant of sand dunes in western France and Jersey. It has lanceolate leaves with 3 to 5 veins.

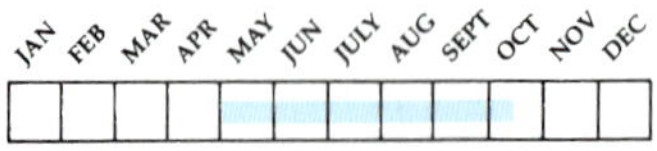

BUCK'S-HORN PLANTAIN

Plantago coronopus

Characteristics: A low-growing, downy biennial, growing up to 10cm tall. The narrow, single-veined, strap-shaped leaves have pinnate lobes, which often curve back. They form a flat open rosette. In some specimens the lobes are reduced to shallow teeth. The short, cylindrical flowerhead is held erect. The minute flowers have a brown corolla and yellow stamens.

Range and habitat: Distributed all around the coast of the British Isles and also some inland areas in the south. Mostly coastal in Europe. A plant of cliff tops, sandy grassland and gravelly soils near the sea. It also occurs on sandy roadsides inland and heaths.

Similar species: Sea Plantain, *P. maritima*, is a plant of saltmarshes and damp coastal habitats as well as mountain streams in the north and west. Also on limestone in western Ireland. It has unlobed, more erect leaves with 3 to 5 veins. The flower spike is usually longer.

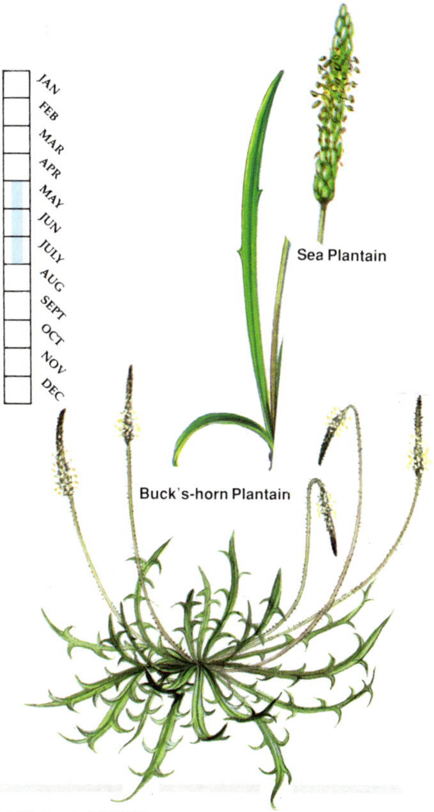

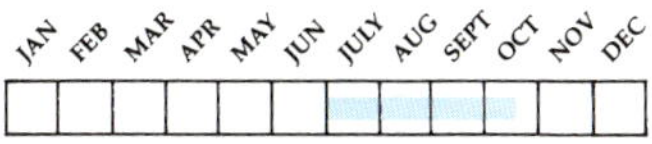

SEA ASTER

Aster tripolium

Characteristics: A fleshy, erect maritime perennial, up to 100cm tall. The leaves are oval to lance-shaped with long tapering stalks and a noticeable central vein; the stem leaves are narrower. The upper half of the plant is branching with loose heads of Michaelmas Daisy-like flowers. The ray florets are typically mauve and the disc-florets, yellow. In some populations the ray-florets are absent.

Range and habitat: Found all around the coast of the British Isles and Europe. A classic plant of the lower margins of the saltmarsh and estuary creeks; also found less frequently along cliff edges.

Similar species: The closely related, Michaelmas Daisy, *A. novi-belgii*, was imported from North America as a garden plant in the 18th Century and has become established in the wild in waste places. They are usually larger than Sea Aster and without the fleshy leaves.

MAN-MADE HABITATS

Nearly all the landscape in Europe, except for high mountain tops and cliff edges, have been radically affected by the hand of man. Even wild moors and heaths are the result of prehistoric clearing of the original post-glacial tree cover, and the most remote woodlands have had their structure altered by centuries of management. But some habitats cannot even be called semi-natural as they are almost entirely the creation of man – city centres, ornamental parks, arable fields, rubbish tips, etc. However, wild plants have colonised these new niches successfully over the centuries, often despite the best attempts of man to exclude them!

Arable weeds are a highly successful group of annual plants, many with almost cosmopolitan distributions as man has unwittingly introduced their seed wherever he has cultivated the land. They are often characterised by having several generations a year, each producing prodigous quantities of seed that can remain viable for long periods, so that any new opportunities can be exploited. This ability is often vividly demonstrated when a new road is cut through arable land – the exposed soil, which for once is not rigorously treated with herbicides, suddenly blossoms into a carpet of poppies and mayweeds. Despite this, some arable weeds which are more susceptible to modern treatments are now becoming increasingly rare.

Waste ground in cities and towns supports its own range of unusual alien plants such as Japanese Knotweed, Canadian Fleabane, Oxford Ragwort and Buddleia, whilst some 'country plants' such as Fat Hen and Scarlet Pimpernel have moved in to take advantage of the new habitats. Scarlet Pimpernel can produce up to 12,000 seeds from one plant and is quick to take advantage of the tiniest patch of bare ground. Other plants, such as Field Bindweed, can survive in areas where the soil is constantly being disturbed by having extremely persistent rhizomes which can produce a new plant from even the smallest fragment. Any gardener with this plant will testify to its exasperating tenacity.

Poppies and Corn Marigolds

COMMON POPPY

Papaver rhoeas

Characteristics: A familiar, upright hairy annual, up to 60cm tall. The leaves are pinnately lobed with toothed segments. The leaves on the upper stem are smaller, stalkless and often 3-lobed. The large red flower is up to 7cm across and crumpled in bud; the petals have a dark blotch at the base. The petals often fall within a day of flowering but a single plant can produce up to 400 flowers throughout its life. The seed capsule is hairless and oval-shaped with a flat top.

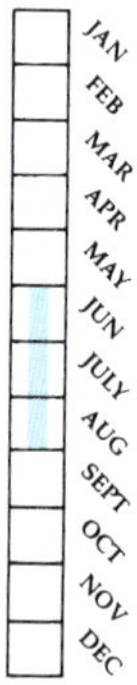

Range and habitat: Common and sometimes abundant in England; less common in Wales and Scotland. An arable weed notably of cereal crops, and of disturbed ground along roads and wasteland on well-drained soils.

Similar species: The red-flowered poppies are best told apart by their seed capsules. Rough Poppy, *P. hybridum*, has a round capsule covered with bristles. Prickly Poppy, *P. argemone*, has a long capsule again covered in bristles and Long-headed Poppy, *P. dubium*, has a long hairless capsule.

GREATER CELANDINE

Chelidonium majus

Characteristics: An erect, branching perennial member of the poppy family, growing to 90cm tall. It is poisonous and exudes a bright orange latex if cut. The grey-green leaves are pinnately lobed; the leaflets have rounded teeth. The bright yellow flowers have 4 oval petals and yellow stamens. They are small (20-25mm across) and are in terminal clusters. The seed capsules are narrow and 3-5cm long.

Range and habitat: Widespread throughout much of the British Isles but most common in the south. Found throughout Europe. Widely used as a medicinal herb for centuries. There is some doubt whether it is native to the British Isles. It is found most frequently near habitations, often along roadsides, hedgebanks and by old walls.

Similar species: The Welsh Poppy, *Meconopsis cambrica*, has much larger yellow flowers (50-75mm across) and has yellow latex.

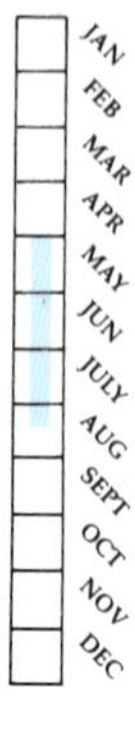

CHARLOCK

Sinapsis arvensis

Characteristics: An erect, hairy annual member of the cabbage family, growing up to 80cm tall. The lower leaves are large with a few small side lobes and a much larger toothed terminal lobe. The stem leaves are shorter stalked or stalkless and narrower. The yellow flowers are in a loose terminal cluster, which elongates in fruit. The flowers have 4 petals and 4 spreading narrow sepals.

Range and habitat: An abundant arable weed found throughout most of the British Isles except for parts of the north of Scotland. Found throughout Europe. Found in crops, field edges and roadsides and prefers heavy soils.

Similar species: Rape, *Brassica napus*, is widely grown for its oil and as a fodder crop and is a now a common weed of roadsides and field edges. It has lobed, oblong, lower leaves and upper leaves that clasp the stem. The buds usually overtop the pale yellow flowers, whereas in the closely related, Wild Turnip, *B. rapa*, the flowers overtop the buds.

HEDGE MUSTARD

Sisymbrium officinale

Characteristics: An erect, branching, bristly annual to biennial, growing up to 90cm. The leaves are pinnately lobed with the toothed lower lobes often pointed backwards. The flowering side-branches are held stiffly, frequently at right angles to the main stem. The flowers are small and yellow and are borne in a terminal cluster which elongates as the fruits ripen. The narrow fruits overlap and are pressed close to the stem. The wiry stems of the plant often persist through winter.

Range and habitat: Found throughout the British Isles, although scarce in parts of northern Scotland. Common throughout Europe. A sometimes abundant weed of field edges, roadsides, hedgebanks and gardens.

Similar species: Eastern Rocket, *S. orientale*, is a native of the Mediterranean that has become widely naturalised over much of northern and central Europe. It has a triangular-shaped terminal lobe to the leaf and long fruits (4-10cm) which are not pressed against the stem.

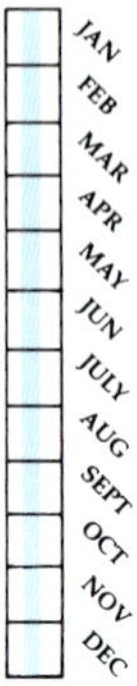

SHEPHERD'S PURSE

Capsella bursa-pastoris

Characteristics: An erect, sometimes hairy annual, growing up to 40cm tall. The basal rosette of leaves is very variable, ranging from pinnately lobed to entire; overall shape is elliptical to strap-shaped. Stem-leaves are also variable, but typically lance-shaped with two pointed basal lobes clasping the stem. The flowers are tiny (2.5mm across) and white in a flat-topped terminal cluster, elongating in fruit. The erect fruits are on long stalks (5-20mm) held almost at right-angles to the stem. The seed capsules are shaped like an upright heart or old-fashioned purse.
Range and habitat: Widespread and often abundant weed found throughout Britain and Europe. A plant of open habitats, including field edges, gardens, waste ground and roadsides.
Similar species: Field Penny-cress, *Thlaspi arvense*, has clasping stem leaves but lacks the basal rosette. The flowers are slightly larger and the fruits are almost circular with a notch at the top.

FIELD PANSY

Viola arvensis

Characteristics: A variable, branching annual, growing up to 45cm tall. The leaves are deeply lobed to unlobed and are roughly oval in shape with large leaf-like toothed stipules. The flowers are carried singly on long stalks and are like a miniature garden pansy, 8-20mm across, and predominately yellow, sometimes tinged blue. The green, pointed sepals are longer than the petals.
Range and habitat: A common arable weed found throughout the British Isles but less frequent in the north and west. Widespread in Europe. Found along field edges and waste ground.
Similar species: Wild Pansy, *V. tricolor*, is also an annual of arable fields, although a subspecies, ssp *curtisii*, is a perennial of coastal dunes and dry grassland. The flowers are larger (15-25mm across); typically the upper petals are blue, the middle, cream and the lip, yellow, but it can be very variable. The sepals are shorter than the petals.

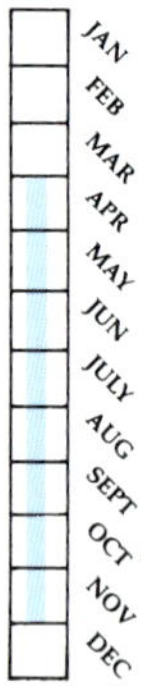

COMMON FUMITORY

Fumaria officinalis

Characteristics: A low-growing, branching hairless annual, up to 40cm tall. The pale waxy-green leaves are 2- to 4-times pinnately divided with flat, lobed leaflets. The flowers are in dense spikes that elongate in fruit. The individual flowers are roughly tubular-shaped, up to 8mm long, with a blunt spur. The overall colour is pink with the petals tipped dark purple. The fruits are globular.

Range and habitat: Widespread and sometimes abundant throughout the British Isles, although less common in the west. Throughout Europe. A scrambling weed of dry soils in open conditions such as field edges, gardens and waste ground.

Similar species: There are many similar species. The White Ramping-fumitory, *F. capreolata*, is a taller climbing plant with white flowers with red tips. It is a common plant of arable fields, old walls and gardens, particularly in the south-west.

BLADDER CAMPION

Silene vulgaris

Characteristics: An erect, hairless perennial, up to 90cm tall. The waxy-green leaves are in opposite pairs and are elliptic, with those near the base stalked and those higher up unstalked. The white flowers are in loose branching clusters. The flower has 5, notched, white petals and a large, veined, inflated calyx.

Range and habitat: Widespread throughout the British Isles but local in north and west Scotland. Found throughout Europe. A common plant of open habitats, such as arable fields, waste ground, grassland and roadsides, particularly on well-drained basic soils.

Similar species: Sea Campion (see p. 122) also has an inflated calyx but the opening is wider. Also it produces a dense mat of non-flowering shoots. Both Sea Campion and Bladder Campion have 3 styles whilst White Campion has 5 styles.

fruit

ANNUAL PEARLWORT

Sagina apatela

Characteristics: A prostrate, rosette-forming annual growing up to 10cm. The stems are thread like with opposite pairs of narrow pointed leaves. The flowers are carried at the ends of the branching stems forming a loose cluster. The tiny petals soon fall leaving the 4 blunt green sepals. The flower-stalks are hairy and sticky. The fruit is as long as the spreading sepals.

Range and habitat: Widespread throughout the British Isles; rarer in the far north. Found throughout Europe from southern Scandinavia southwards. A common plant of bare ground and other open habitats such as garden paths, walls and roadsides on well-drained, sandy soils.

Similar species: There are several other species of pearlwort but the one most likely to be encountered is the Procumbent Pearlwort, *S. procumbens,* which has a distinct non-flowering rosette, which produces rooting stems from which the flowering shoots arise. Forms a dense bright green, moss-like mat. The fruit is longer than the sepals.

COMMON CHICKWEED

Stellaria media

Characteristics: A sprawling, branching, almost hairless annual, stems growing up to 40cm. The rounded stems have a single line of hairs which changes side after each leaf junction. The heart-shaped to oval pointed leaves are stalked near the base and stalkless and more crowded near the tip. The small flowers have 5, deeply notched, white petals with the green hairy sepals equal in length. The reddish-brown fruits are rounded.

Range and habitat: Widespread throughout the British Isles and Europe. A common and sometimes abundant weed of arable fields, gardens, roadsides and waste ground, particularly on broadly neutral, fertile soils.

Similar species: The much less common Greater Chickweed, *S. neglecta,* is larger with stems up to 90cm long. It typically has 10 stamens as opposed to Chickweed which has 3 to 8. It is a plant of damp woodlands and streamsides.

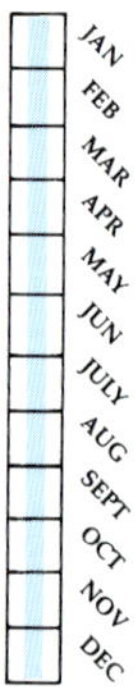

CORN SPURREY

Spergula arvensis

Characteristics: A weak, scrambling annual, growing up to 30cm. It is covered in sticky hairs. The narrow strap-shaped leaves are in distinct whorls and are fleshy with a channel below. The white flowers are in a loose, branching, terminal cluster. The long stalks are erect in flower but turn down in fruit. The flower itself has 5, oval petals which are longer than the pointed, green sepals. The flowers only open during the afternoon.
Range and habitat: A widespread arable weed found throughout much of the British Isles and Europe. It is a plant of arable fields and field edges on dry sandy soils. In Britain, it used to be grown as a fodder crop up until the 16th century but is now considered a troublesome pest. It is still grown to supplement sheep and cattle feed in some parts of the Continent.
Similar species: None.

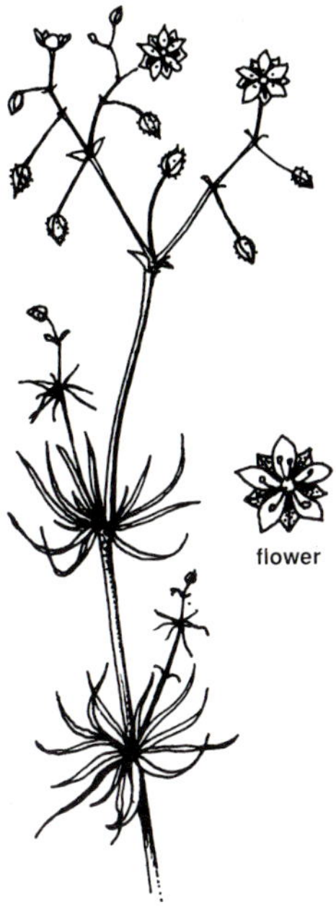

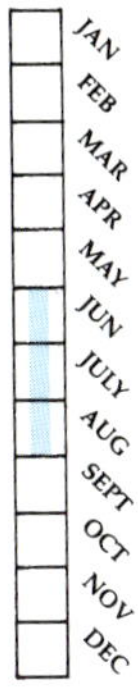

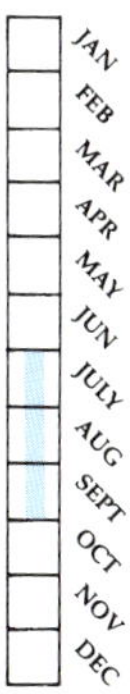

FAT HEN

Chenopodium album

Characteristics: An upright, annual with a mealy surface giving it a grey-green colour; grows up to 100cm tall. The stem is angled, often having a red-dish tinge in mature specimens. The lower leaves are diamond-shaped in outline with the 2 upper sides toothed. The upper leaves become more lance-shaped towards the tip. The flowers are held in dense erect spikes, and are a grey-green colour with 5 segments. For many centuries it was grown as a vegetable crop.
Range and habitat: Found throughout the British Isles, although less common in northern Scotland. Widespread in Europe. An abundant weed of arable fields, waste ground, gardens and roadsides, particularly on fertile loams.
Similar species: Good King Henry, *C. bonus-henricus*, has distinctly triangular leaves, typically untoothed. The flowers are in a long, terminal, leafless spike. Often found growing in enriched soils. Formally cultivated. See also Common Orache overleaf.

COMMON ORACHE

Atriplex patula

Characteristics: A sometimes erect, branching, mealy-coloured annual, growing up to 100cm. The leaves vary from diamond-shaped near the base to lance-shaped higher up. The lower leaves are distinctly toothed, the bottom pair of teeth often pointing forwards. The flowers are in dense, leafy spikes consisting of both male and female flowers. The male flowers are almost globular and have 5 segments rather like a *Chenopodium* but the female flowers are enclosed by two green leaf-like bracteoles.

Range and habitat: Widespread in the British Isles except the north of Scotland. Found widely in Europe. A plant of arable fields, waste ground and open habitats, particularly near the sea.

Similar species: Spear-leaved Orache, *A. prostrata*, is found in similar habitats and can be told by its triangular leaves with the two outside lobes pointing outwards rather than upwards. It is typically not as mealy as Common Orache. There are several other oraches with narrower leaves.

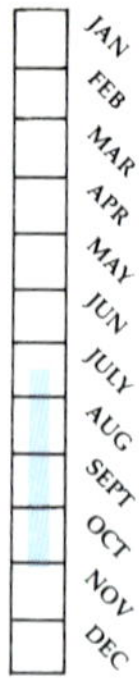

COMMON MALLOW

Malva sylvestris

Characteristics: A hairy, branching, often spreading perennial, growing up to 90cm. The long-stalked, crinkly leaves are palmately-lobed and toothed. Upper leaves more deeply lobed. The large flowers (up to 4cm across), consist of 5, notched, narrow, rose-purple petals, with dark purple veins. The fruits are in a central disc and shaped like little cheeses. It is a relative of the cottage-garden hollyhocks and hibiscus and has long been valued for its medicinal properties.

Range and habitat: Widespread and common in Britain north to southern Scotland; rare in most of Scotland. Found throughout Europe. A plant of hedgebanks, roadsides, field edges and waste ground usually on well-drained soils. Its deep tap root means that it is able to withstand dry conditions.

Similar species: Musk Mallow, *M. moschata*, is also a plant of roadsides. It has rounded basal leaves and finely dissected stem leaves. The flowers are paler and smaller than Common Mallow.

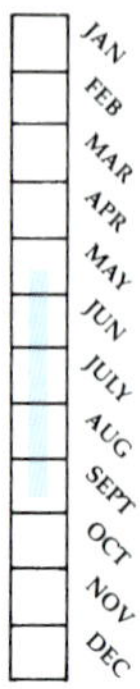

BROOM

Cytisus scoparius

Characteristics: A bushy, deciduous shrub, growing up to 2m. The stems are spineless and green with 5 angles. The stalked leaves have 3 oval leaflets, soon falling. The large, pea-like, yellow flowers are up to 20mm. The pea-like pod turns black and has brown hairs on the margins. Broom was long thought to have magical powers and was the emblem of the Plantagenet kings. It was also used as a diuretic and was often used to sweep the floors!

Range and habitat: Found throughout almost all of the British Isles. Widespread in Europe from Spain to southern Scandinavia. A plant of well-drained soils along roadsides, waste ground and acid grassland.

Similar species: Spanish Broom, *Spartium junceum*, is a plant of southern Europe now widely introduced in France and southern England. It is taller with a rounded stem and flowers later in the year.

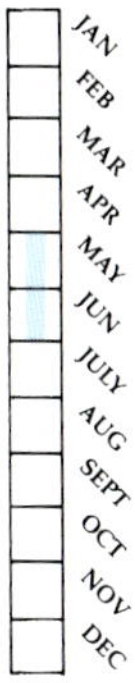

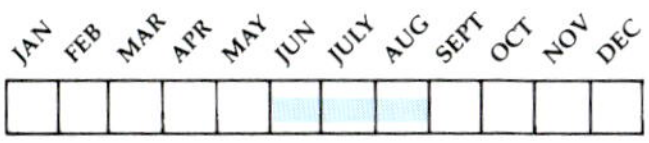

SILVERWEED

Potentilla anserina

Characteristics: A prostrate, creeping perennial with distinct silvery-green foliage, typically forming extensive mats by means of its runners. The leaves are pinnate with 7 to 12 pairs of main leaflets, which are deeply lobed and particularly silky on the underside. The bright yellow flowers, up to 20mm across, are on long stalks and have 5 petals. The roots of this hardy plant were once eaten by crofters in Scotland and Ireland.

Range and habitat: Found throughout the British Isles, except for parts of northern Scotland. Widespread throughout most of Europe. A common plant of trackways, roadsides, sand dunes and waste ground.

Similar species: It is told from the other *Potentilla* species by the ground-hugging mats of silvery, pinnate leaves.

AGRIMONY

Agrimonia eupatoria

Characteristics: A slender, upright, hairy perennial, growing up to 60cm tall. The leaves are pinnate, with 3 to 6 pairs of main toothed leaflets alternating with smaller ones; the leaflets are longer towards the tip of the leaf. The flowers are in a long, terminal, leafless spike. The individual flowers are small (5-8mm across) with 5, yellow petals. The fruits are covered in hooked bristles which catch on to passing animals, walkers and botanists, so dispersing the seed.

Range and habitat: Widespread throughout the British Isles but most common in the south. Found throughout most of Europe. A plant of well-drained soils alongside trackways, roadsides and waste ground as well as rough pasture and scrub.

Similar species: Fragrant Agrimony, *A. procera*, is a more local plant with ungrooved fruits; also the outer bristles of the fruit are turned back.

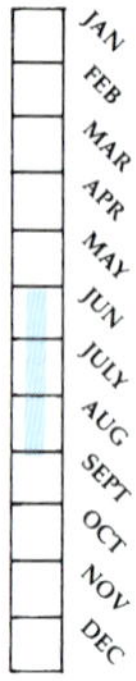

WHITE STONECROP

Sedum album

Characteristics: A succulent, evergreen perennial, creeping or erect, growing up to 15cm tall. The leaves are egg-shaped and bright green, 6-12mm long, typically not adpressed to the stem. The 5-petalled white flowers are in a branching terminal cluster, drooping in fruit. The term stonecrop derives from this group of plants' habit of growing in stony ground.

Range and habitat: A common plant in most of Europe, particularly to the south. Its status in Britain is uncertain; although it may be native in southern regions, it is probably introduced in most of the British Isles. It is a locally common plant of old walls, paths and buildings.

Similar species: The English Stonecrop, *S. anglicum,* is also a white flowered stonecrop and can be a common plant in coastal regions. It has red-tinged leaves and the flowerhead is less branched than White Stonecrop.

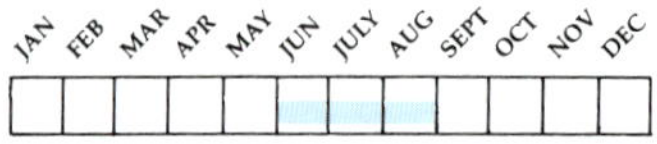

COMMON EVENING-PRIMROSE

Oenothera biennis

Characteristics: A tall, downy, biennial member of the willowherb family, growing up to 100cm tall. The leaves are lance-shaped and hairy, basal ones stalked, stem leaves shortly stalked or unstalked with a red mid-rib. The flowers are large (up to 50mm across) in a leafy spike. They consist of 4, broad, yellow, overlapping petals. The flowers open in the evening and are pollinated by moths. The fruits are long, narrow, pod-like capsules.

Range and habitat: A native of North America, it was introduced in the 19th Century and is now widely naturalised in both Europe and southern Britain, although it appears to be decreasing. It is not found in Ireland. A colourful plant of roadsides, waste ground and other well-drained open habitats.

Similar species: There are several other Evening-primrose species that have become established. The most common is the Large Evening-primrose, *O. erythrosepala*, which is found in similar habitats and has larger flowers.

GROUND ELDER

Aegopodium podagraria

Characteristics: An erect, hairless perennial member of the carrot family, growing up to 100cm tall. It is able to spread vigorously by means of its creeping rhizomes. The leaves are broadly triangular in outline and have long-stalked oval, pointed, toothed leaflets. The flat-topped umbel of white flowers is terminal with 15 to 20 rays, with no bracts or bracteoles.

Range and habitat: Originally introduced into Britain from the Continent many centuries ago it has now spread to most of the British Isles, except northern Scotland. A widespread woodland plant on the Continent. In Britain it is a notorious weed of gardens, roadsides and hedgebanks.

Similar species: The distinctive elder-like leaves and the absence of bracts and bracteoles should distinguish it from other umbellifers.

FOOL'S PARSLEY

Aethusa cynapium

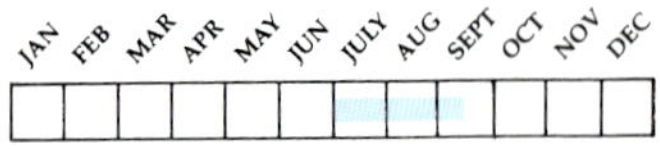

Characteristics: An erect, branching, hairless, poisonous, annual member of the carrot family, growing up to 50cm tall. The stem is hairless and round, slightly ribbed and tinged reddish towards the base. The leaves are very like Cow Parsley, being 2- to 3-pinnate. The flat-topped umbel of white flowers is distinctive in that it has no bracts but long, narrow, spreading bracteoles. The fruits are globular and ridged. It flowers in mid-summer, typically much later in the year than Cow Parsley. Fool's Parsley is well worth knowing as it is extremely poisonous and can be lethal.

Range and habitat: Widespread in southern Britain but rarer in the north and west. Found throughout Europe. A common weed of arable land, gardens and waste ground.

Similar species: The long, narrow bracteoles together with the absence of bracts should distinguish it from other umbellifers.

HEMLOCK

Conium maculatum

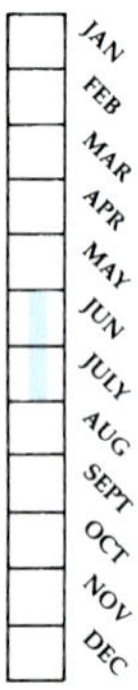

Characteristics: An erect, hairless, biennial member of the carrot family, growing up to 2m tall. The grey-green hollow stem is conspicuously purple-spotted. The large leaves are finely dissected, 2- to 3-pinnate, with toothed leaflets. The umbels of white flowers are borne at the ends of side shoots and the top of the plant. The rays have a few small bracts and bracteoles on the outer side of the umbels. The fruits are globular with ridges. The plant has an unpleasant smell if bruised. It is highly poisonous.

Range and habitat: Widespread throughout the British Isles, although more local in the far north and Ireland. Found throughout Europe. A plant of roadsides, streambanks, waste ground, usually on damp fertile soils.

Similar species: The height, smell and greyish purple-spotted stems are highly distinctive; however, if you are unsure, stay well away from this poisonous plant.

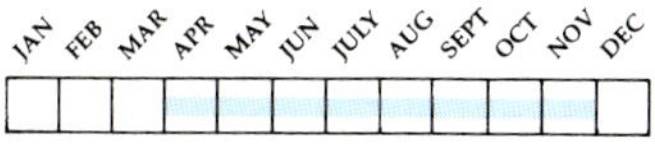

SUN SPURGE

Euphorbia helioscopa

Characteristics: An upright, hairless annual, growing up to 50cm. The typically unbranched, round stem has alternate, stalkless leaves with a tapering base and broader, blunt tips, which are finely toothed. The flowers are in a 5-rayed umbel-like branching head, with a ruff of 5, large, leaf-like bracts at the base. The flowers, which have neither petals or sepals, are surrounded by small, rounded, leaf-like inflorescence-glands, which are tinged yellow. The globular fruits are green and smooth.
Range and habitat: Widespread throughout most of the British Isles, although more local in northern Scotland. Found throughout Europe. A common weed of arable land, field edges, gardens and other open habitats, particularly on base-rich soils.
Similar species: The other spurge of this habitat that is most likely to be encountered is the Petty Spurge, *E. peplus*. The leaves of this smaller plant are untoothed and more oval in shape and the flowerhead is typically 3-rayed.

KNOTGRASS

Polygonum aviculare

Characteristics: A prostrate or ascending, branching annual, sometimes forming large mats. Leaves are lance-shaped and untoothed, larger on the main stem, with a papery sheath-like stipule at the junction with the stem. The 1 to 6 tiny flowers arise from leaf-junctions and are very shortly stalked with no petals and a 5-lobed calyx tinged rose-pink or white at the tips. The 3-sided fruits are dark brown and slightly larger than the calyx.
Range and habitat: Widespread throughout the British Isles but local or absent from parts of the north of Scotland. An abundant weed of arable land, waste ground, shorelines, roadsides and gardens.
Similar species: Equal-leaved Knotgrass, *P. arenastrum*, is a prostrate plant of waste ground and paths; it has equal-sized leaves on both the main and the side branches.

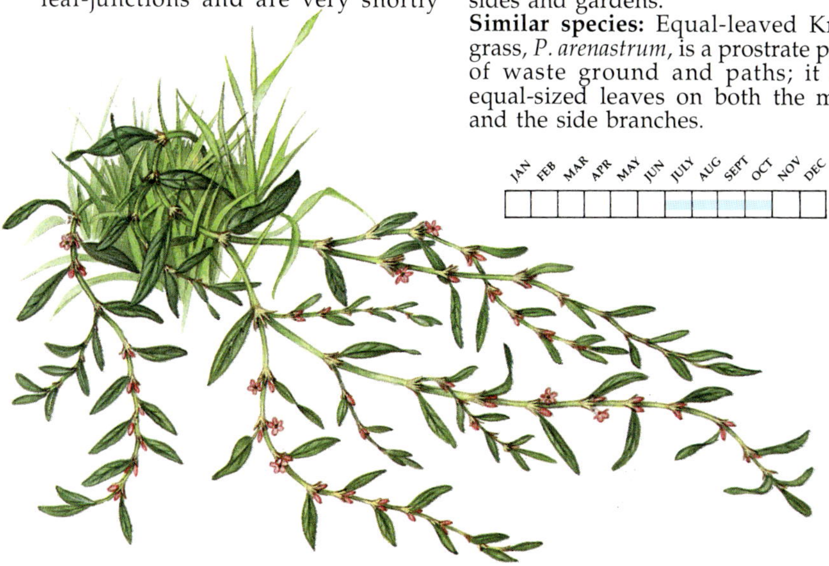

JAPANESE KNOTWEED

Reynoutria japonica

Characteristics: A robust, hairless perennial, growing up to 2m, often forming dense stands by means of vigorous rhizomes. The stout stems are tinged reddish and change direction at each leaf junction producing a zig-zag effect. The leaves are large (up to 12 x 10cm), broadly oval with a short, pointed tip and a wedge-shaped base. The panicles of flowers arise from the leaf axils and are up to 10cm long. The flowers are dioecious and dull white.

Range and habitat: A native of Japan, introduced into Britain in the early 19th Century as a garden plant. During this century it has become widely established as a garden escape, frequently turning up on rubbish dumps, waste ground, streamsides and roadsides, where its extensive root system makes it difficult to eradicate. It is most frequent in the west of Britain.

Similar species: Giant Knotweed, *R. sachalinesis*, is an even larger garden escape, growing up to 3m tall. The large leaves gradually taper into a point.

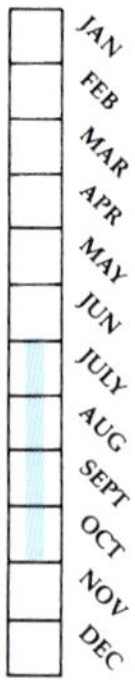

BLACK-BINDWEED

Fallopia convolvulus

Characteristics: A prostrate or scrambling annual, with long, mealy, twining stems, up to 120cm long. The widely-spaced, arrow-shaped or bindweed-like leaves are up to 6cm long; there is a silvery sheath at the junction with the stem. It typically twines clockwise around surrounding plants unlike true bindweeds which twine anti-clockwise. The tiny greenish flowers arise from the leaf-axils and are in short spikes.

Range and habitat: Found throughout the British Isles except for parts of the north of Scotland. Widespread and common throughout Europe. A common weed of arable land, gardens, waste ground and roadsides.

Similar species: The more local Copse-bindweed, *F. dumetorum*, is confined to scattered sites in the south of Britain, although more widespread on the Continent. It is a taller plant with longer fruiting stalks.

CURLED DOCK

Rumex crispus

Characteristics: An erect, robust perennial, growing up to 100cm tall. The long, lower leaves (up to 30cm) are oblong to lance-shaped with a rounded or tapering base. The edges are distinctly wavy or crisped, hence the name. The small, green flowers are in dense leafy spikes, arising from upright side branches and are terminal. The fruits are distinctive and are often the best way of identifying species of dock; this species has 3 green wings without teeth, with reddish swellings or warts on each side of the fruit.

Range and habitat: Widespread and common throughout the British Isles and Europe. A weed of a wide range of conditions from arable land and gardens, to disturbed grassland, waste ground, beaches and watersides.

Similar species: Broad-leaved Dock, *R. obtusifolius*, is also a very common dock of disturbed ground and can be very persistent. It has broader leaves with heart-shaped bases, and fruits with clearly toothed wings and only one side with a large swelling.

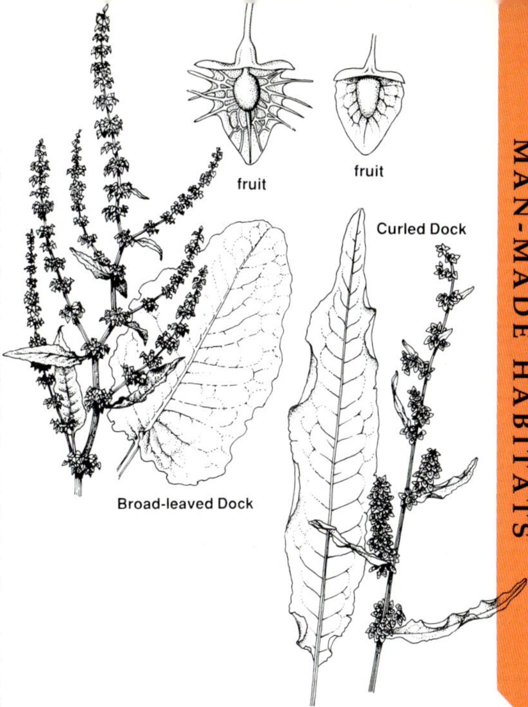

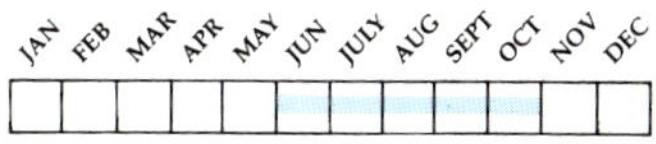

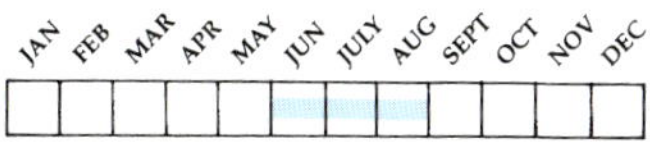

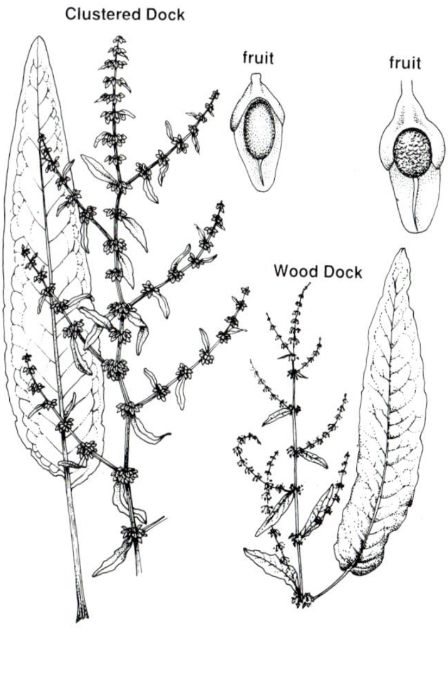

WOOD DOCK

Rumex sanguineus

Characteristics: An erect, branching perennial, up to 100cm tall. The lower leaves are broadly lance-shaped with rounded bases; occasionally red-veined. The leaf stalks are up to half as long as the leaf. The flowers are in interrupted whorls, which have leafy bracts only towards the base. The side branches are typically at an acute angle to the main stem. The 3-sided fruits do not have toothed edges and only have one round swelling.

Range and habitat: Widespread throughout much of the British Isles, including Ireland, but less common in Scotland and absent from parts of northern Scotland. A plant of woodland rides on clay soils and also waste ground, roadsides and commons.

Similar species: Clustered Dock, *R. conglomeratus*, is similar but the flowering branches are typically held at a wider angle from the main stem. The leaf stalk is roughly the same length as the leaf and the fruit has an oblong swelling on each side.

STINGING NETTLE

Urtica dioica

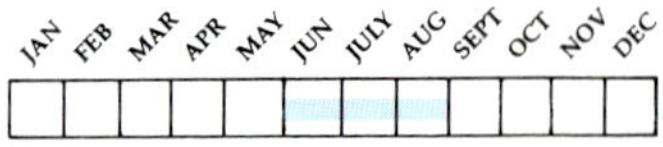

Characteristics: An erect, bristly perennial, growing up to 150cm, covered in stinging hairs. Often forming dense clumps by means of its thick, creeping rhizomes. The long-stalked opposite leaves are roughly triangular, with rounded, heart-shaped bases and are coarsely toothed. Plants are dioecious, i.e. male and female flowers are on separate plants. The small, green female flowers are held in drooping clusters arising from the leaf axils; the male flowers are held in shorter more stiff clusters. It is wind pollinated.

Range and habitat: Found throughout the British Isles and Europe. A common and sometimes all too abundant plant of fertile soils. As well as being a weed of waste ground, roadsides, field edges and gardens it can be found in fens and damp woods.

Similar species: The Small Nettle, *U. urens*, is a local annual. It grows up to 50cm tall and has more oval-shaped leaves, sometimes shorter than the stalks.

SCARLET PIMPERNEL

Anagallis arvensis

Characteristics: A prostrate or scrambling, hairless annual, growing up to 30cm long. The stems are 4-angled. The oval, pointed leaves are in stalkless pairs along the stem. The flowers arise singly on long, slender stalks from the leaf axils. The flower consists of a spreading 5-lobed corolla, with the petals usually overlapping and fringed with minute hairs, and can vary from blue through pink to white but is most typically red. The pointed calyx lobes are only just shorter than the corolla. The flowers open only during the morning and early afternoon when it is sunny, hence its other name of Shepherd's Weather-glass.

Range and habitat: Widespread throughout the British Isles but more coastal in Scotland. Found throughout Europe. A common weed of arable land and roadsides on lighter soils.

Similar species: The Blue Pimpernel has corolla lobes that do not overlap and are sparsely fringed with hairs. It is a more local southern plant.

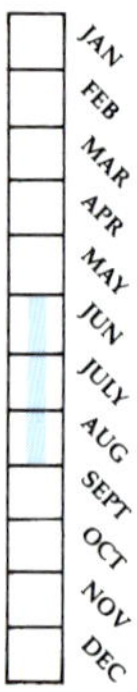

FIELD BINDWEED

Convolvulus arvensis

Characteristics: A prostrate or climbing perennial, growing up to 75cm long. The shoots, which twist anti-clockwise, arise from persistent, white rhizomes. The alternate leaves are 2-5cm long and arrow-shaped with the two basal lobes sometimes curling upwards. The funnel-shaped flower is up to 3cm across and white, pale pink or striped with both colours. The calyx is 5-lobed and the fruit globular.

Range and habitat: Found throughout southern Britain, local and absent from parts of Scotland and Ireland. Widespread in Europe. A troublesome weed of arable land and gardens, where it can be difficult to eradicate because of the deep rooting rhizomes. Also found along roadsides, waste ground and coastlines.

Similar species: Told from the *Calystegia* species such as Sea Bindweed, *Calystegia soldanella*, as it does not have bracts covering the calyx.

BLACK NIGHTSHADE

Solanum nigrum

Characteristics: An erect or branching annual, growing up to 60cm. It is related to the potato and is poisonous. The leaves are oval and pointed, with a wedge-shaped base and toothed edges. The potato-like flowers are in loose side-clusters and have 5, white, spreading corolla lobes and yellow anthers. The fruit is a large, round berry, at first green, later turning a shiny black. The plant has been used for medicinal purposes in the past but is highly poisonous, containing an alkaloid, solanine. The potato, *S. tuberosum*, except for its tubers (when they are not green) is also poisonous.

Range and habitat: Found throughout southern England, local in Wales and south-western England, rare in the north and absent from Scotland and Ireland. Throughout Europe; one of the world's most widespread arable weeds. A weed of arable land, gardens and waste ground, particularly on fertile soils.

Similar species: Green Nightshade, *S. sarrachoides*, is an naturalised plant from Brazil, which is increasing in southern areas. It has a similar appearance to Black Nightshade except the berry is green and it has an enlarged calyx.

COMMON TOADFLAX

Linaria vulgaris

Characteristics: An erect, slender, hairless perennial, growing up to 80cm tall. The greyish-green leaves are strap-shaped (up to 8cm); the lower leaves are in whorls, the higher leaves are alternate. The flowers are in a tall terminal spike. The bright yellow flower is irregularly shaped, rather like a thin snapdragon flower. There is a distinctive raised orange area at the entrance to the 'mouth'. The base of the flower has a long pointed spur. The shape of the flower means that it is mostly pollinated by bumble-bees.

Range and habitat: Widespread in Britain as far north as central Scotland. Local in Ireland. Found widely in Europe. A familiar summer plant of roadsides, waste ground and field edges on well-drained soils.

Similar species: Pale Toadflax, *L. repens,* has pale purple flowers with a short spur. It is a more local plant of stony, dry soils.

IVY-LEAVED TOADFLAX

Cymbalaria muralis

Characteristics: A pretty, trailing, hairless perennial, with stems up to 80cm long. The small (2.5cm), ivy-shaped leaves are on long stalks, and are often tinged purplish. The flowers are on long, upward curving stalks and are like miniature snapdragons, coloured lilac. There is a white opening to the 'mouth',with a yellow spot at the centre. The spur is short and curved. In fruit the stalk curves down until it reaches the wall surface, where the capsule can be pushed into a crack.

Range and habitat: A native of the Mediterranean, it was first introduced in to England in the 17th Century. It has since spread to most parts of the British Isles except for the north of Scotland. It is especially common in the south-west. A plant typically of old walls and less often on rocks.

Similar species: The habit and ivy-shaped leaves make this a highly distinctive species.

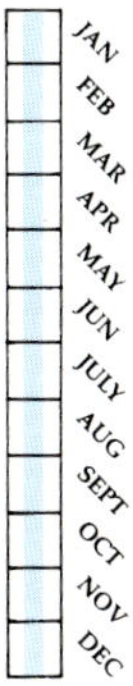

WALL SPEEDWELL

Veronica arvensis

Characteristics: A small, hairy, often stiffly erect annual, growing up to 25cm. The leaves are roughly oval and coarsely toothed; lower leaves stalked. The flowers are in a long, leafy, terminal spike. The flowers have very short stalks and the corolla is clear blue. The fruit capsule is hairy and round to heart-shaped and approximately as long as the spreading sepals.
Range and habitat: Found commonly throughout almost the whole of the British Isles and Europe. A common weed of open arable land, gardens, dry grassland and sometimes old walls.
Similar species: The upright habit, hairy, toothed leaves and all blue flowers, which are shorter than the calyx should tell it apart from other speedwells. The Ivy-leaved Speedwell, *V. hederifolia*, is a common creeping plant with long-stalked, broadly heart-shaped, lobed leaves and pale lilac, stalked flowers. The fruits are round and hairless.

COMMON FIELD SPEEDWELL

Veronica persica

Characteristics: A sprawling, hairy annual with prostrate and semi-erect stems. The leaves are triangular- to oval-shaped, coarsely toothed and stalked. The flowers arise from the leaf-axils on long stalks which are noticeably longer than the leaves when in fruit. The corolla is blue with a white lower lip. The broad, hairy fruit has 2 spreading lobes with sharp ridges.
Range and habitat: A native of western Asia, it was first introduced to Britain at the beginning of the 19th Century and is now widespread over much of the British Isles except for some parts of Ireland and Scotland. It is found throughout Europe from southern Scandinavia southwards. It is an abundant weed of arable land, gardens and waste ground.
Similar species: Grey Field Speedwell, *V. polita*, is less common and has an all blue corolla and rounded fruit, with short hairs. Green Field Speedwell, *V. agrestis*, has the rounded fruit but has a white lower corolla lobe like Common Field Speedwell.

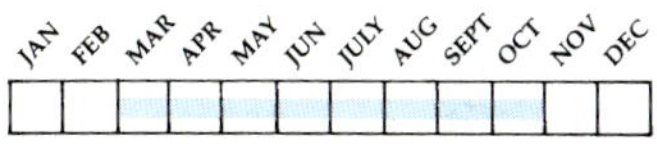

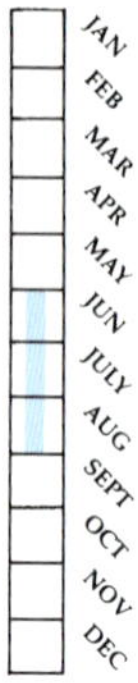

RED BARTSIA

Odontites verna

Characteristics: An erect, branching, downy annual, growing up to 50cm tall. The stalkless leaves are lance-shaped with a few teeth. The flowers are in leafy spikes on upper side-branches, which can be acute or almost at right angles to the main stem, and are also terminal on the main stem. The flowers, which all face the same direction, are small with a tube-like pink corolla ending in 2 lips, the lower one of which has a darker reddish patch and 3 lobes; the upper lip is hooded. It is semi-parasitic on grass roots.

Range and habitat: Widespread throughout the British Isles and most of the continent. A common plant of tracksides and field edges as well as permanent grassland, and waste ground.

Similar species: Yellow Bartsia, *Parentucellia viscosa*, as its names suggest, is a sticky, yellow-flowered plant of coastal regions. It is confined to the southwest in Britain but is more widespread in western France southwards to the Mediterranean.

COMMON BROOMRAPE

Orobanche minor

Characteristics: A member of the wholly parasitic family, the Orobanchaceae, which do not produce their own chlorophyll but take their nourishment from the roots of other 'host' plants. Common Broomrape, is an erect, unbranched, downy plant growing up to 50cm. The stem is a reddish or purplish colour with a few brownish scales. The flower spike is terminal. The scale-like bracts are the same length as the flowers; the curving corolla tube is yellow with purple veins. The stamens are more or less hairless.

Range and habitat: The most common broomrape. Widespread throughout England and Wales, particularly in the south-east. Rare in Ireland and northern England. Absent from Scotland. Common on the Continent northwards to Belgium. Parasitic on clovers and occasionally on other members of the pea family, very rarely on other plants.

Similar species: There are a number of other similar species but it is often easier to determine them by identifying the host species.

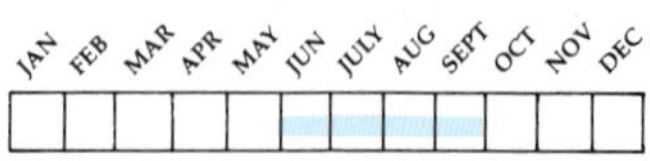

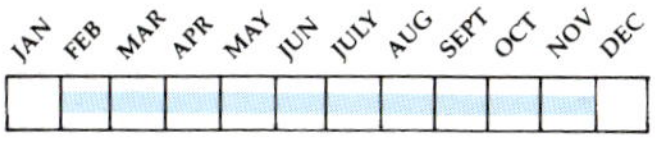

RED DEAD-NETTLE

Lamium purpureum

Characteristics: A downy annual, frequently branching from the base, growing up to 45cm. The stems are 4-angled and typically tinged reddish, particularly in mature specimens and often bare below the flower spike. The leaves are long-stalked, oval with a heart-shaped base and coarse, rounded teeth; often tinged reddish like the stem. The flowers are in a dense terminal series of whorls, with shorter stalked leaf-like bracts. The flowers are pink. The tubular corolla has a hooded upper lip and a lower lip consisting of 2 short side-flaps and a toothed central lobe dotted with darker spots.

Range and habitat: Widespread and often abundant throughout the British Isles except for parts of north-west Scotland and Ireland. Found throughout Europe except the Mediterranean. A plant of waste ground and cultivated land everywhere.

Similar species: Henbit Dead-nettle, *L. amplexicaule*, has brighter flowers in more distant whorls and stalkless upper leaves.

WHITE DEAD-NETTLE

Lamium album

Characteristics: A hairy, erect perennial, growing up to 60cm tall, and often forming dense clumps by means of its creeping rhizome. The pointed, oval leaves and bracts are up to 7cm long, stalked and coarsely toothed resembling Stinging Nettle leaves but without the sting, hence the common name 'dead-nettle'. The striking flowers are in whorls along the top half of the stem and are white with 2cm long corollas with a large hooded upper lip and a smaller 3-lobed lower one. The flower is pollinated mainly by bees.

Range and habitat: Widespread in Britain; common in the south and east becoming increasingly rare towards the north and west. Absent from parts of Scotland. Found throughout most of Europe. A familiar wild flower of field edges, gardens, roadsides, waste ground and hedgebanks.

Similar species: Unmistakable in flower.

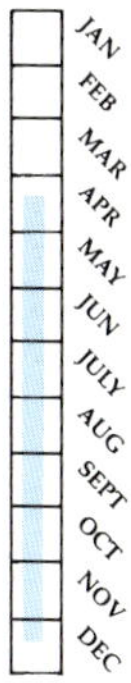

COMMON HEMP-NETTLE

Galeopsis tetrahit

JAN	FEB	MAR	APR	MAY	JUN	JULY	AUG	SEPT	OCT	NOV	DEC

Characteristics: A bristly, erect, branching annual, growing up to 100cm. The stems have red-tipped, glandular hairs particularly below the swollen nodes. The coarsely-toothed, pointed leaves are in opposite pairs and oval in shape, tapering towards the stalk. The flowers are in whorls up the stem. The flower itself has a calyx with 5, long, bristly teeth; the corolla is often pinkish with a hooded upper lip and a lower one with 3 spreading lobes; there is a series of dark spots at the base of the centre lobe.
Range and habitat: Widespread throughout the British Isles and Europe. A common plant of cultivated land but also found in damp woods and fens.
Similar species: There are, in fact, two very similar species which can only be told apart by careful examination of the flower. Large Hemp-nettle, *G. speciosa,* is a larger more branching plant with a yellow corolla and purple central lobe to the lower lip.

JAN	FEB	MAR	APR	MAY	JUN	JULY	AUG	SEPT	OCT	NOV	DEC

GREATER PLANTAIN

Plantago major

Characteristics: An erect, sparsely downy perennial with flower stalks up to 45cm (more usually 10-20cm) tall. The leaves are in a flat to semi-erect basal rosette. They are oval to elliptical with parallel veins; the leaf blade narrows suddenly into a long leaf stalk which is about as long as the leaf. The dense, greenish, cylindrical flowerhead is on a an erect, unfurrowed, leafless central stalk. The tiny flowers (3mm across) have an off-white corolla and anthers which are purple at first, later yellow. It is wind pollinated.
Range and habitat: Found almost throughout the British Isles and Europe; indeed, it seems to have followed the progress of Europeans around the world. A common plant of well-trampled open habitats such as pathways, roadsides and waste ground; it is a persistent weed of lawns.
Similar species: Ribwort Plantain (see p. 74) has semi-erect, lance-shaped leaves and a taller flowering spike. Hoary Plantain (see p. 75) has scented flowers and has a shorter stalk.

FIELD MADDER

Sherardia arvensis

Characteristics: A hairless, low, spreading annual, with stems up to 40cm long. The stems are 4-angled with minute backward-pointing bristles along the ridges. The leaves are in whorls of 4 to 6 along the stem and are elliptical with tiny forward-pointing bristles on the underside and edges. The flowers are in a tight cluster of 4 to 8 in terminal heads with a ruff of leaf-like bracts below. The flowers themselves are tiny (3mm across) and funnel-shaped with 4 flat lobes at the mouth; the corolla is a lilac colour. The 4 to 6 green sepals persist in fruit.

Range and habitat: Widespread in England, Wales and Ireland becoming more coastal in Scotland. Originally a native of the Mediterranean it is now found throughout most of Europe. At one time it was cultivated for a red dye that could be extracted from the roots. It is a plant of cultivated land on light, well-drained soils.

Similar species: Told from other members of the bedstraw family by its clusters of lilac-coloured flowers.

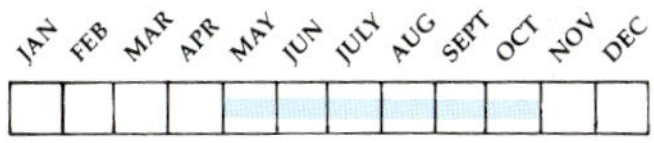

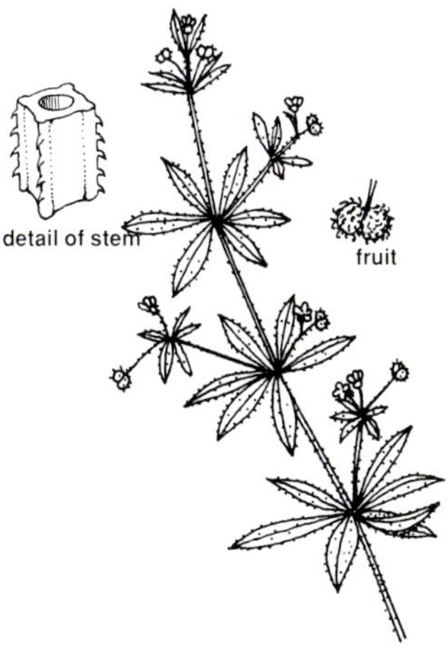

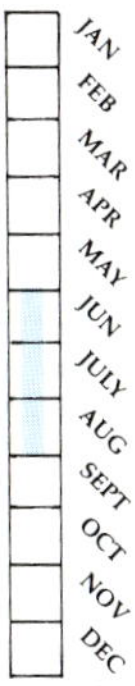

GOOSEGRASS

Galium aparine

Characteristics: A more or less hairless, sprawling annual, with branching stems up to 120cm long. The stems are 4-angled with tough, backward-pointing bristles or hooks along the ridges. The leaves are in distinct whorls of 6 to 8 along the stem; the single-veined leaves are strap- to lance-shaped with backward-pointing bristles along the edges. The tip is pointed, with a spine. The tiny, white, 4-lobed flowers are in small, branched clusters arising from the leaf axils. The fruits have 2 globular capsules covered with white hooks which readily catch on to passing animals and people, hence one of its other names, Cleavers. The name Goosegrass comes from the former practice of feeding the plant to geese.

Range and habitat: Found throughout the British Isles and most of Europe. A common and sometimes abundant plant of hedges, waste ground, roadsides and scrub on fertile soils.

Similar species: Told by its size, the backward-pointing prickles on the stem and leaves and the hooked fruits.

RED VALERIAN

Centranthus ruber

Characteristics: An attractive, erect, hairless perennial, up to 80cm tall. The stem and leaves are a grey-green colour. The leaves are oval to lance-shaped in opposite pairs up the stem; the lower leaves are shortly stalked, the upper ones are sessile and occasionally join around the stem. The flowers are in dense, red (sometimes white), terminal, branching panicles. The flowers are tubular (10mm long) with 4 flat lobes at the end with a single protruding stamen and a spur at the base. The ripe seed has a pappus of feathery hairs. The flower is pollinated by long-tongued butterflies and moths.

Range and habitat: A native plant of the Mediterranean, now frequently naturalised in much of Britain as a garden escape. Particularly common in the south-west. Also naturalised throughout much of the Continent.

Similar species: The near relative, Common Valerian, has pinnate leaves.

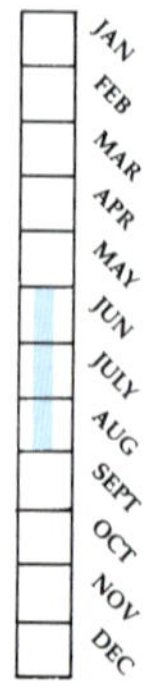

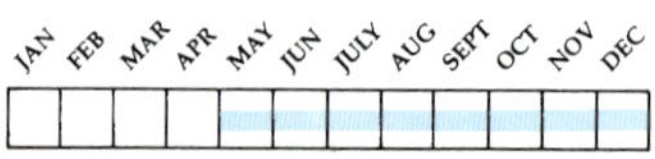

OXFORD RAGWORT

Senecio squalidus

Characteristics: A spreading, bushy, almost hairless annual, sometimes perennial, member of the daisy family, up to 30cm tall. The leaves are glossy green, once or twice pinnate with narrow, pointed leaflets. The lower leaves taper into a stalk; upper leaves clasp the stem. The yellow flowerheads are in loose, branching clusters, each up to 20mm across, with an inner disc of tightly packed florets and an outer circle of about 13 strap-like ray florets. The bracts on the receptacle below are all conspicuously tipped with black. The seed has a pappus of hairs.

Range and habitat: A native of mountain areas in the Mediterranean it escaped from the Oxford Botanic Gardens at the end of the 18th Century and is thought to have spread along the newly made railway system. It is now a common plant of railways, waste ground and roadsides in England and Wales. It has also spread to many other European countries.

Similar species: See Common Ragwort, (p. 77).

GROUNDSEL

Senecio vulgaris

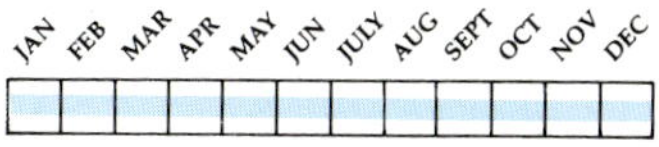

Characteristics: An erect,branching, usually hairless annual, growing up to 45cm tall. The stem is fleshy and sometimes tinged purplish. The distant leaves are irregularly pinnately-lobed and oblong in shape; the lower leaves are shortly stalked, the upper leaves clasp the stem. The flowers are in dense clusters at the ends of the branches and main stem. They later become more open as the flowerhead stalks elongate. The flowerheads have only tiny yellow disc florets. The cylindrical receptacle has an outer row of black-tipped bracts. The seed has a long, white, feathery pappus.

Range and habitat: Found throughout the British Isles, except for the Scottish Highlands, and nearly all of Europe. An abundant weed of cultivated areas, including gardens and field edges. Also found along roadsides and waste ground, particularly on heavy soils.

Similar species: Heath Groundsel, *S. sylvaticus,* is a taller plant of woods and heaths on sandy soils. It has very short ray florets.

COLT'S-FOOT

Tussilago farfara

Characteristics: One of the earliest flowering members of the daisy family to flower, providing a bright splash of golden yellow along roadsides early in the year. It is a low, hairy perennial, with flowering shoots, up to 15cm tall, arising from creeping stolons. The leaves, which are not fully developed until after the plant has flowered, are round- to heart-shaped, distantly toothed with a downy surface below; they can become large, up to 20cm across. The flowers are solitary on erect, leafless stalks, covered with purplish-tinged bracts; they close during dull weather. The flowerhead initially droops in fruit, later becoming upright to disperse numerous seeds with feathery white papuses.

Range and habitat: Found throughout the British Isles and most of Europe. An abundant weed of arable land, roadsides, waste ground and dunes. Most common on heavy soils.

Similar species: None.

MARSH CUDWEED

Gnaphalium uliginosum

Characteristics: A low-growing, densely woolly, annual branching from the base, and growing up to 15cm tall. The stems and leaves have a felt-like surface giving the plant a grey-green colour. The leaves are strap-shaped, narrower at the base, the upper leaves forming a ruff below the dense cluster of 3 to 10 flowerheads and the ends of the leaves overtopping them. The flowerheads have brown, woolly bracts and yellowish florets.

Range and habitat: Found throughout the British Isles but less common in northern Scotland and parts of Ireland. A common plant of damp or partially flooded areas, mostly on acid soils, often found along damp field margins, pond edges, heaths and roadsides.

Similar species: There are a number of other low-growing cudweeds, many of which have local distributions. Common Cudweed, *Filago vulgaris*, is widespread on dry acid soils and has an erect habit with distinct branching stems near the top.

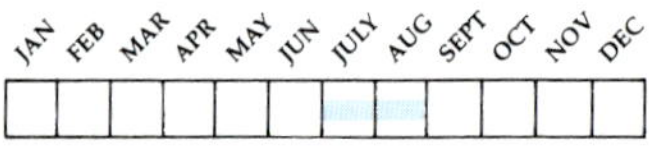

CANADIAN FLEABANE

Erigeron canadensis

Characteristics: An erect, sparsely hairy, annual, growing up to 100cm. The numerous stem leaves are strap-shaped and spirally arranged up the stem. The top part of the plant is very branched, with ascending flowering branches forming a dense panicle of flowerheads. Each small, white flowerhead (up to 5mm across) is borne singly at the end of a branch and consists of both disk and short ray florets. The seed has a yellowish pappus of hairs.

Range and habitat: A native of North America, it was first introduced to Europe about 200 years ago. It is now found throughout most of England and parts of Wales, though it is most common in south-east England. Rare elsewhere. A plant of waste ground and roadsides where it can be abundant, especially on well-drained soils.

Similar species: Blue Fleabane, *E. acer*, is a native plant of grasslands and dunes on well-drained soils. It is a shorter plant with pale blue, ray florets and is less branching.

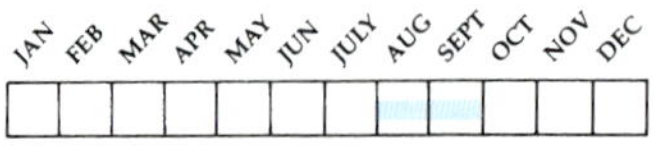

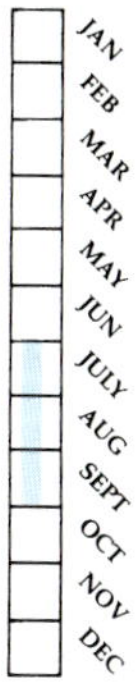

ross-section of flower

SCENTLESS MAYWEED

Tripleurospermum inodorum
(=*Matricaria maritima*)

Characteristics: A low-growing, branching, hairless annual (sometimes perennial), growing up to 60cm tall. The leaves are broadly oblong in outline and are 2- to 3-times pinnate with narrow strap-shaped leaflets. The stem and leaves have a grey-green colour. The flowerheads are in loose panicles and are solitary at the ends of long stalks. Each flowerhead is up to 4.5cm across, with a disc of dense yellow disc florets and up to 30 white, strap-shaped ray florets. The seeds do not have feathery pappuses.
Range and habitat: Widespread and common throughout most of the British Isles. Widespread in central and northern Europe. A common weed of arable land, waste ground and roadsides on well-drained soils.
Similar species: A member of a confusing group whose classification is constantly changing. Scented Mayweed, *Matricaria recutita*, looks similar but the flowerhead is hollow in fruit.

PINEAPPLEWEED

Matricaria matricarioides

Characteristics: A low-growing, erect, hairless annual, growing up to 30cm. The leaves are dark green and smell of pineapples if bruise. The leaves are oblong in outline and are 2- to 3-times pinnate with narrow, strap-shaped leaflets. The flowerheads are held solitarily on short branching stalks. They have a dome of greenish-yellow disc florets and no ray florets. The bracts around the receptacle have a broad papery margin. The seeds do not have feathery pappuses.
Range and habitat: Thought to be a native of north-east Asia but now established widely around the world. First found in Britain in Wales in 1871 and has since spread to most areas. It is widespread throughout Europe. A common weed of waysides, field gateways, roadsides and waste ground. Tolerant of trampling.
Similar species: The lack of ray florets and the strong scent make it relatively easy to identify.

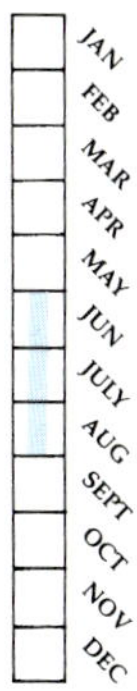

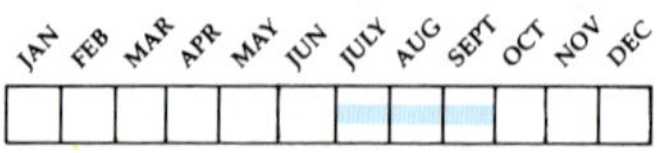

LESSER BURDOCK
Arctium minus

Characteristics: A large, thistle-like, erect, hairy biennial, growing up to 130cm tall. The stem is grooved and woolly. The leaves are large (up to 40cm long) and roughly oval-shaped with a heart-shaped base. The leaf stalk is hollow. The flowerheads are in loose leafy spikes. The oval to globular flowerhead has a receptacle covered in hook-tipped spines and a narrow crown of purple florets. The seed has a short pappus of white hairs.

Range and habitat: Found throughout the British Isles except for parts of northern Scotland. Widespread in Europe. A plant of waste ground, hedgebanks and woodland edges.

Similar species: Greater Burdock, *A. lappa*, looks very similar but the lower leaf stalks are solid and the leaves are as wide as they are long. The flowerheads are always globular and have long stalks.

SPEAR THISTLE
Cirsium vulgaris

Characteristics: An erect, spiny biennial, growing up to 150cm tall. The stems are covered with cottony hairs and have interrupted spiny wings. The leaves are lance-shaped in outline with pinnate lobes and a wavy, toothed margin covered in strong spines. Stem leaves have a long terminal lobe; they are cottony and spiny on the upper surface. The flowerheads are 2 to 3 in a loose cluster or solitary, oval-shaped and up to 4cm wide with a receptacle covered in spiny bracts, the outer ones of which are spreading and the florets reddish-purple. The seed has a pappus of white feathery hairs.

Range and habitat: Widespread and abundant throughout the British Isles and most of Europe. A familiar weed of field-edges, roadsides, neglected pasture and waste ground, particularly on fertile soils.

Similar species: Told from other thistles by the combination of a spiny stem and leaves with bracts that have outward pointing spines. Creeping Thistle has unarmed stems and lilac florets.

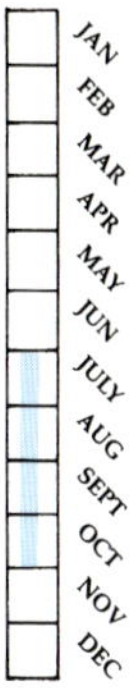

PERENNIAL SOW-THISTLE

Sonchus arvensis

Characteristics: A large, erect, hairy perennial, growing up to 150cm tall and forming patches by means of creeping rhizomes. The large stems are grooved and covered in glandular hairs towards the top, cottony below; hollow. The plant exudes a milky juice if cut. The large leaves are roughly lance-shape with pinnate lobes; weak spines on the edges. The basal leaves have short, winged stems; the upper leaves clasp the main stem. The flowerheads are in loose terminal clusters, are large (up to 5cm across) and dandelion-like. The receptacle is bell-shaped and covered in yellowish sticky hairs. The seed does not have a pappus.

Range and habitat: Widespread throughout the British Isles and Europe. Found along field edges, river banks, waste ground and saltmarshes.

Similar species: Smooth Sow-thistle, *S. oleraceus*, is similar but has a smooth stem, the leaves have pointed basal lobes and the flowerhead is a pale yellow. Prickly Sow-thistle, *S. asper*, has thistle-like, wavy, spiny leaves.

DANDELION

Taraxacum officinale

Characteristics: A familiar low-growing perennial, with flowering stalks typically up to 30cm tall. There are over 200 microspecies of dandelion, many of which are highly difficult to separate. The main features of the group are as follows. The leaves are in a flat, basal rosette arising from a long tap-root. The plant exudes a milky juice if cut. The leaves are pinnately lobed and lance-shaped; the lobes are typically pointed. The flowerheads are solitary on hollow, fleshy, leafless stalks arising from the centre of the rosette. The flowerhead is golden yellow, with a wide-spreading head of florets. The seed has a white pappus, forming the familiar 'dandelion clock'.

Range and habitat: Widespread and often abundant throughout the British Isles and Europe. An ubiquitous group of plants found in a wide range of habitats.

Similar species: One of our most familiar plants but one that can also keep a botanist puzzled for a long time if he or she wants to identify it precisely.

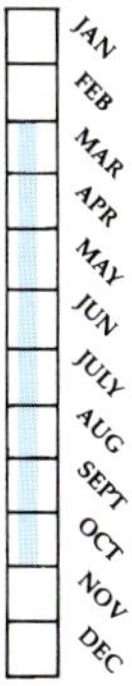

INDEX